THE VERY GOOD LIFE

A YORKSHIRE SAGA

by

MARGARET SUNLEY

HUTTON PRESS

1987

Published by the Hutton Press Ltd.
130 Canada Drive, Cherry Burton, Beverley
East Yorkshire HU17 7SB

Printed by Clifford Ward & Co.
(Bridlington) Ltd.
55 West Street, Bridlington
East Yorkshire YO15 3DZ

ISBN 0 907033 56 3

To my husband, Cyril,
without whom this book
could not have been written.

INTRODUCTION

This is the story of a more than middle-aged couple, a York schoolmistress and her husband, who forsook their comfortable town-life to try the "good life," before the good-life became the thing to do.

The book has moments of pathos, but also episodes which are hilariously funny. Animals are like people, believes the author, each with its distinctive character, to be treated as individuals, not lumped together in a herd.

MARGARET SUNLEY
Bridlington
May 1987

Front cover photograph by Martin Sunley

CHAPTER ONE

"Do you think he's dying?" I murmured, as Cyril and I stood in the goat-house, watching Billy struggling for breath.

"Yes, but I don't know what we can do," sighed my husband. We felt helpless as we watched his strength ebbing away. It had happened so rapidly as to be almost unbelievable. The previous evening, he had been his usual magnificent self. I don't use the word 'magnificent' lightly. Billy was an outstanding specimen of goathood, weighing all of twelve stones and standing about three feet high at the shoulder. His white hair and beard were long and silky and, despite his great size and strength, he was as gentle as a kitten. Indeed, he was the only goat I've ever known who answ red to his name and actually came when called.

We had owned him now, for about a year — a year in which we'd become very fond of the gentle Billy. Our herd of nanr ies had gradually expanded until it was clear that we needed our o /n billy-goat, as no one in the district seemed to possess one. W 'd been several weeks combing the 'Livestock' columns in the local paper, before seeing an advert for, not one, but two billy-goats for sale. As we didn't possess a trailer, Cyril removed the back seat from the car, with the idea of using it as an estate car, of sorts. It was this that was the eventual reason for our choice of Billy, rather than the alternative goat. The old lady who owned them had treated them as pets, taking them for daily walks on a lead, until she was reluctantly forced to part with them due to arthritis. This regime accounted for their good nature.

Faced with the two goats, I rather leaned towards the 'British Alpine,' as he was a smaller and daintier goat. The 'Saanan,' which was Billy, was so huge that I could see problems, when he came to serve our young goatlings. However, the decision was made for us. Marmaduke's horns sprang from his head in two great sweeps, and there was no possible way he could be accommodated in the back of the car, so, Billy it had to be.

The main obstacle was to physically get him into the car. It was a two-door Capri, and the problem of persuading him to enter the door and clamber into the rear seemed daunting, to say the least. Frail and old though she was, however, his owner certainly knew her goats.

The magnificent Billy.

"'E's very fond of oak leaves," she volunteered, "go-o o'er theere an' pull some twigs off yon tree."

Obligingly, I did as directed, while Cyril held on to the goat's collar. I then opened both doors and folded forward the backs of the front seats. The rear of the car was already swathed in old blankets so, with everything prepared, I waved my twigs enticingly in front of Billy, gradually retreating towards the car. Unfortunately, mistaking size for slowness, my retreat was too gradual and, with a sudden jerk forward, which almost floored Cyril, he demolished the whole supply of twigs before my plan had even begun to work. Back I trudged across the paddock and returned, laden this time with a great armful from the oak trees. Some of these I placed inside the car, and then began my stratagem once more.

Craftily keeping most of them just out of his reach and allowing him to nibble just a few, I retreated, managing to keep just ahead of the munching jaws. When I felt the car against my spine, I groped with one hand for the doorway and backed into it. This was no mean feat, with the huge animal pressing forward, eager to devour my load. Now I was bent double in the back of the car with my feet feeling round for a way out, avoiding the pit-falls of folds of blanket and the bump in the floor where the drive-shaft, or something, goes.

With his head inside the car, the goat seemed to have second thoughts about actually entering. Cyril tried a shove, but he might as well have pitted his strength against a Sherman tank. We seemed for a moment to have reached an impasse, so I dangled the oak leaves under his nose, to lure him to follow me. Now came the tricky bit.

There was no room for the three of us, so Cyril was forced to release his hold on the collar. Let's face it, there was no room for two of us! As Billy's front feet climbed into the car and the huge head was pushed enquiringly towards me, I scrambled backwards in a crouched position, desperately wondering what would happen if I tripped. Happily, I managed my reverse out of the car without mishap and, as Billy's back legs lumbered in, I slammed the door in his face. He looked quite hurt at this rebuff and, when Cyril, just as quickly, did the same with his door, the goat was left in possession, looking puzzled, but still placidly chewing the oak leaves.

While Cyril paid the owner, I opened my door a fraction and pushed my seat upright. This effectively trapped Billy in the back, whereon I found it safe to open the door fully and sit in. I pushed Cyril's seat back, ready for him, and heard the old lady's voice.

"'E's never been for a ride before. I 'ope 'e likes it."

"Now she tells us," I thought.

Cyril got into the driving seat and so began the oddest ride I've ever experienced. If you've never travelled in the front seat of a car, with a mature, fully-grown billy-goat occupying the back, you've never savoured life to the full.

Make no mistake, a billy-goat, at any time of the year, is not the most fragrant travelling companion. Luckily, it was not autumn or the inside of the car would have been unbearable, not only that day but for weeks afterwards. Things weren't improved when, having eaten the oak leaves and twigs, he turned his attention to my hair. Not that he actually tried to eat it — he just nuzzled and nibbled at it in an absent-minded way, while looking round the car with thoughtful appraisal.

To say that he'd never travelled before, except on his own four legs, he took it all very calmly. Cyril kept the car at a sedate pace, so as to disturb Billy's equilibrium as little as possible, but he couldn't actually have been thrown about, as his back seemed to be quite firmly wedged on the car roof. As he was unable to hold his head upright, he stood with it bowed, but turned sideways, chewing my hair.

"Crikey!" Cyril shouted suddenly, looking in the wing mirror. "That's all we need!"

Try as I might, I could see nothing behind, but the goat's bulk. "What's the matter?"

"A police car on our tail."

Those words rouse a feeling of unease in even the most law-abiding citizen. We certainly weren't speeding. Was our licence up to date? Perhaps there was some obscure law against transporting goats in cars. We hadn't bothered to check up. Our fears were groundless, it appeared. As they drew alongside, we could see both officers were doubled up with laughter, and the passenger gave us a mock salute as they passed. Was it merely coincidence that they slowed down and drove in front of us for some miles? Was Billy the only goat to have had a police escort? However, to our relief, and with a final wave, they turned right as we turned left, at the next crossroads.

When we reached home, Billy descended from the car, with all the dignity of the Queen Mother being handed out of a state landau. Cyril may as well have been a minion, preceding him through the domain, rather than his master leading him to his new quarters, such was the majesty with which he strolled through the garden. The tethered nannies bleated comments to each other as their new lord and master passed them, but he merely eyed them speculatively as he made his august way to his supper. We felt that Billy was too ordinary a name for such a regal creature. Perhaps we should rename him King William. However, Billy he was, and Billy he remained.

Thus it was that Billy entered our lives, which were all the richer for knowing him. For all his great size, he was the least trouble of any of our goats. As I've said, he would come at a gallop when his name was called and then stand obediently to have his collar put on. I had to put both arms round him to fasten it, so thick was his neck. If we had been able to buy or make one, he would have been ideal for pulling a goat-cart, being both strong and yet docile. The best we could do was to lift our three-year-old grand-daughter, Tammy, on his back, and let her ride him like a pony. Cyril even made a harness and reins, which Billy seemed to enjoy wearing, and she spent many

Tammy on Billy's back.

happy times riding her unusual mount. On one occasion, and I'm sure it was a joke, he stopped dead in his tracks and she catapulted over his head, to somersault into a heap of lawn cuttings. He'd chosen the spot well, that's why I think it was a joke on his part. The toddler was unhurt and rolled in the grass, chuckling, while he prodded her with his nose, to get up again.

These games, of course, could only proceed in certain months of the year. Once the mating season started, we realised that the stories of the pungency of goats were not exaggerated. Before we invested in our own Billy, we had been warned of the strength of the smell, but this was worse than we could possibly have imagined. The trouble was, of course, he was such an affectionate animal and couldn't understand why we had suddenly stopped stroking and petting him. The more we backed away, the more he wanted to press and rub against us, to express his devotion.

Before going to town, Cyril would bathe or shower and change every article of clothing and yet his progress through a shop or supermarket was met with sniffs and muttered comments about drains or even stink-bombs. No matter how careful he was, the smell was impossible to eradicate and our son, Martin, usually greeted

11

him with, "Ugh, Dad! You've been with that stinking old billy-goat again!"

I'm afraid it was an occupational hazard over five months of the year. He had his own quarters, away from the nannies, otherwise he would have made the milk taste strong. Those not yet in-kid would be presented to him morning and evening, like concubines paraded before a Sultan. We advertised his services in the local paper and, in addition to his own harem, he had a constant procession of in-season nannies calling for his services. He really lived the life of Riley and his fame spread throughout the area.

When out shopping, we were often accosted in the street by faintly-familiar folks, asking "How's Billy?"

If we appeared not to know them, we were reminded.

"He's the father of my Heidi," or "Lucy," or some other goatling.

Now, looking sadly down at him, it seemed that his life as a stud-goat was finished. In fact, it looked as though he could not live for another hour, so rapidly was his condition worsening.

It had happened the previous evening, when Cyril was leading him back to his shed. Passing a small rhododendron bush, he had snipped off a mouthful of leaves. We had known, when we first began to keep goats, that rhododendron was poisonous to them, but it was a particularly lovely specimen and, as we kept the goats fenced away from this part of the garden, we considered it to be safe, so I had been loath to part with the plant.

Habit had made us careless, and the fact that Cyril had taken a short cut when putting Billy away the previous evening, had led to the calamity. I knew that Cyril was extra-distressed, because he blamed himself for the goat's condition. As soon as he grabbed the leaves, Cyril had prised open his jaws and, as he thought, scooped them all out. However, some, if only a small amount, had evidently been swallowed and, though he had seemed all right when Cyril checked the stock at bed-time, in the morning he refused his food and just stood, with his noble head drooping.

As the day progressed, his condition had deteriorated. After searching through all our goat books, with no luck, Cyril began to ring round all the goat-keepers of our acquaintance, while I made a coat for Billy. The only advice we could find in the books was that any sick goat must be 'rugged,' so, if we could do nothing else, we could at least keep him warm. Consequently, a rug was made out of an old blanket, and strapped around the ailing goat.

12

Meeting with no success through local telephone calls, Cyril rang the vet. After all, Billy was not merely our stud-goat; he was our friend, and we'd move heaven and earth to save him.

The vet's response was like the knell of doom.

"Rhododendron? I'm sorry, but I'm afraid it's fatal. The only thing I can do is to come and put the poor old lad out of his misery."

This seemed so final, that we clung to hopefulness a little longer, though we realised that it was very slim. Besides which, he wasn't writhing in pain, merely growing weaker and sleepier.

"Thank you, but I think he'll probably have gone before you could arrive," Cyril replied miserably.

Throughout the morning, he had grown steadily worse. Now he was lying prostrate, his eyes dull and with not even sufficient strength to raise his head from the ground. All we could do was crouch beside him and stroke his face, murmuring comforting phrases. Cyril suddenly got up.

"I'll try old Herbert. He used to keep a lot of goats. In fact, he was a Goat-Judge at shows."

It was an inspiration. 'Old Herbert' had never personally known a goat who'd suffered from rhododendron poisoning but: "I have heard of a potion that's supposed to work."

Cyril ran back, clutching a piece of paper. "Have you these things?" he demanded.

"Lard? Yes. Bicarb? Yes. Black treacle? No — I've only Golden Syrup. Will that do?"

"I don't know. We'd better have it right. As it is, he wasn't sure about the quantities."

After unsuccessfully trying the village shop for black treacle, Cyril set off to bring some from Pocklington, some six miles away. After putting a block of lard to melt in a pan over a very low heat, I went back to my vigil. Poor Billy tried to lift his head to look at me, but his strength failed and it dropped back on to the straw. All I could do was stroke his face and watch him grow weaker.

It seemed no time at all before I heard the car and Cyril was back, with his tin of black treacle. He must have driven like a maniac to have been there and back in such a short time. By now, the lard had melted, so we added a generous dollop of the treacle and stirred them together. Cyril brought a large lemonade bottle and we examined the gooey mess in the pan, unsure of exactly when to add the bicarb, or how much. However, there was no time to waste, so I tipped in what I thought was a fair amount. The result was unexpected. The whole, dark-brown toffee-like mass fizzed up and overflowed all over the cooker. Snatching the pan from the stove, I went over to the table, where Cyril was holding a funnel in the bottle-neck. As soon as it was half-full, we set off for Billy's shed.

Propping the bottle up in the manger, I helped Cyril to try to get the goat on to his feet. By now, he was too weak to help, and no matter how we strained and pushed, we couldn't move the great body. In the end, Cyril raised Billy's head and propped it up by shuffling his own knees under it. As he opened the goat's jaws, and tipped his head back, I put the bottle into his mouth and poured the contents down his throat. Luckily, he was able to swallow the revolting mixture but, no sooner was it down, than back it came!

Before Cyril could leap out of the way, the goat began to retch and heave, spewing the contents of his stomach over his trousers. For a split second, all his affection for Billy fled, but then he realised that this may be the life-saver we wanted.

"Good!" he said, which was magnanimous, considering the mess he was in. He then disappeared out of the door.

When I'd moved all the soiled straw from round the goat, I went for some water to clear his beard and neck, only to find my husband outside the back door in his underpants. What a blessing we'd put six-foot interwoven fencing round this part of the garden! This sight would have caused raised eyebrows in the village. I was convinced that they already considered us, if not absolutely dotty, at the least, eccentric. Cyril, standing with his trousers in his hand, would confirm their opinion.

"They'll have to go in the bin," as I passed him.

"Well, that's that," I said, as I surveyed my cooker top. The black treacle and lard had now set, and it wasn't a pretty sight, rather like a coating of Bonfire toffee.

"No it isn't! The dose has to be repeated in an hour," he answered as he disappeared upstairs, in search of another pair of expendable trousers.

That hour sped by.

I took a bucket of clean, warm water, and finished cleaning up the goat. Perhaps he looked a little brighter. I wasn't sure.

By the time I'd scraped and washed the gunge from the cooker top, it was time for the next concoction.

"This time there's no lard, just treacle and bicarb."

Well, at least if any other clothes received the goat's offering, they'd perhaps be washable, minus the grease.

Forewarned is forearmed. When the treacle was of a pouring consistency, I took the pan outside before adding the bicarbonate of soda. Learning from the previous error, I put it in slowly stirring all the time, so that the eruption was controlled. This time, the evil-looking brew merely fizzed, darkly, in the ruined pan. What with expendable trousers and expendable pans, this was proving as costly as a visit from the vet. However, we were hopeful that our ministrations might result in a living goat when we were through. No way could the vet have saved him.

We hurried through the orchard and into the goat-house.

"I think he does look a little brighter," said Cyril, hopefully.

I wasn't too sure.

"It's difficult to tell," I observed. I didn't like to cast doubts, but I hardly dare hope.

However, as we crouched down beside him in the straw, he managed to raise his head, to receive the bottle's contents. Perhaps it didn't taste as bad as it looked.

"He couldn't do that an hour ago!" exclaimed Cyril, triumphantly.

At the end of the dose, however, Billy's head drooped wearily on to the straw and, with a faint sigh, he closed his eyes. We weren't sure whether he should have kept it down, or whether it should have come back, like the lard-laced dose. However, we could do nothing about his reaction to the medication — just administer it and hope for the best.

We checked him every hour and, by bed-time, he was breathing more normally and raised his head as soon as we entered.

"I don't feel that I can leave him all night," said Cryil when we went to bed.

"Put the alarm clock on and we'll go and check him at about two o'clock," I suggested.

We hadn't expected to sleep, but we woke with a start when the alarm sounded.

"Don't you bother to come, love," urged Cyril, but I felt I must see for myself how Billy was getting on.

What a blessing the night was mild. We stumbled through the orchard in dressing-gowns and slippers, by the wavering light of a torch. I made a mental note that we needed new batteries.

We opened Billy's door and switched on the light, wondering what sight would meet our eyes. Though by no means a pessimist, I do like to face the worse that can happen, so that I'm sure that I can cope. Now, therefore, I was quite prepared to be confronted by Billy's lifeless body. However, to our delight, not only did he raise his head at our entrance, he actually tried to get up. He managed to straighten his back legs, but remained kneeling on the front ones, just unable to make it.

When presented with a container of rolled oats, though he sniffed and nuzzled them, he didn't actually try to eat. He then turned his head away from them and slowly subsided once again on his side.

We were ecstatic. Though he was by no means out of the wood, it was like a miracle in the few hours since he'd first been dosed. Giving him a pat, we almost skipped back to bed, so much happier did we feel.

We woke up early the next morning hardly daring to hope that we'd really effected a cure, when even the vet had pronounced the rhododendron to be fatal.

We knew, from our contact with goats, that they aren't really hardy animals. Although physically strong, constitutionally they tend to be delicate, and even if we'd managed to pull Billy through his dose of poison, there was still the possibility of him succumbing to pneumonia, caused by the shock to his system.

However, not only was he alive, but looking much better. He greeted our appearance by rising, rather shakily, to his feet and even eating a few of the rolled oats we'd brought to tempt him.

Cyril and I hugged and kissed each other, with joy and relief. I could even have kissed the goat, but restrained myself.

"We've done what the vet and all the books said was impossible. He's going to make it."

Tears ran unchecked down my cheeks, and I turned away, to rub the goat's nose. Cyril put plenty of fresh hay in the rack while I went out and pulled him some leaves of comfrey. Not only were all the goats fond of this plant, but we had great faith in its curative powers.

Suddenly, the reaction set in, and tiredness engulfed me. Looking at Cyril, I could see that he felt the same.

"Come on, lass. We'll go and have breakfast and try to have an easier morning," he said, putting an arm round my shoulders.

"Thank goodness it's Sunday and I can stay at home," I rejoined, turning to look once more at old Billy, who was still on his feet.

16

"We'll leave the coat on him for a day or two," I suggested.

"Good idea," answered Cyril, as he went out of the door. "It'll stop the risk of a chill."

We were greatly touched by the number of telephone calls we received during the next few days, enquiring about Billy. The relief brought by news of his recovery was widespread and heartfelt, and we realised that it wasn't just his future services to their nannies that concerned the callers. They felt genuine affection for the goat, whose character endeared him to all who met him.

Needless to say, the offending shrub was dug up that very day and presented to a grateful, goatless neighbour.

CHAPTER TWO

Cyril, my husband, is a farmer's son and though, early in our marriage, we had been forced to leave farming, love of the land always remains. During more than ten years of enforced exile as reluctant town-dwellers, we had always longed for the day when we could buy our own place in the country, with a bit of land. That was as far as our dreams went. We knew that we'd never be able to afford even a small-holding, but a country cottage with a large garden would be a compromise. Surely that would satisfy the land-hunger which seemed inbred.

Searching the property columns in the local paper had become a habit, and attempts at auctions to acquire the rather dilapidated place which we could 'do up,' had met with no success. We had our heart-stopping moments, of course, when success seemed to be within our grasp. Alas for our hopes! We had always encountered an adversary with more money and who was obviously a more experienced, or confident 'doer-up,' and we'd been pipped at the post or, rather, knocked out with the gavel.

Eventually, of course, every dog has its day and luck changes. Our day came when our daughter, Paula, saw in an estate agent's office window, details of a likely proposition. There wasn't the cliff-hanger of an auction. The property was for sale by private treaty, so it was a case of first past the post. We'd never heard of the village but, according to the blurb, it was only twelve miles from York, so commuting was no problem.

It was a grey day in February when we set off, armed with our permit to view. Before we'd been on the way more than a few minutes, snow began to fall. At first, there were merely a few lazy flakes drifting down, but soon it developed into a fine, driving mist, through which vision was difficult.

"We must be mad," muttered Cyril, squinting through the wind-screen. "Just a minute! There's somebody there. Ask him the way."

We stopped the car and we could just make out a grey shape, hunched against the cold. I wound down the window and poked my head out into the bitter wind.

"Excuse me, are we on the right road for Cottingwith?" I shouted.

"East or West?" came back, faintly through the blizzard. Hurriedly, we searched through the viewing particulars.

"My little grey home in the west."

"East."

"Well, thoo's t'wrong side of t'river," came the laconic reply, as he disappeared into the swirl.

This was about the last straw, and Cyril and I were all for returning to the cosy warmth of home. Somehow, a town-blizzard, bounded by familiar streets, doesn't seem as alien as a country-blizzard, stretching forever into unknown fields.

However, Paula pleaded.

"Go on, Dad," she begged, "We've come so far. We may as well go on."

Upon consulting the map, we found that we were indeed on the wrong side of the river, and the nearest bridge was miles away. When we eventually sorted out the route (with mutterings about women navigators from my right), and found the village, the storm had abated and the place looked quite attractive, under a light covering of snow.

The cottage looked larger than we'd anticipated, but rather more ramshackle than its photograph had led us to expect. It had once, in its prime, been white, but was now a dingy grey and surrounded by almost an acre of very neglected land. We were certainly looking for something 'in need of modernisation and restoration,' as the adverts say, and this one filled the bill.

With Cyril humming the tune of 'My Little Grey Home in the

West,' we went up the path. Though neglected, the house seemed sturdy. The pantiled roof had no apparent sag, and the window frames looked firm enough. The appearance of the cottage was, to our eyes, somewhat spoilt by a modern, glass front door, but that was easily remedied. As we approached, the front door opened and a motherly figure appeared.

"Come in! Come in! It's bitter outside," she welcomed. Our first impressions of it weren't too bad but, as we viewed 'Rose Dene,' it became progressively worse.

It was double-fronted, with a square, nicely-proportioned hall. The left side of the house consisted of a pleasant, cosy sitting room with a tiny kitchen opening off. From this, the back door opened on to the land at the rear. By no stretch of the imagination could it be called a garden. So far, so good.

The right side of the house, downstairs, at any rate, was a different kettle of fish. To begin with, it had never been lived in, never had the benefit of fires and family occupation. The front room, at this side, had been the village shop. Though it had a small bow window, of the 'Quality Street' type, there was little else in the way of charm. The room was lined with peg-board, coloured a drab, mouldy green. The grubby, red cement-floor had two channels, forming an 'L' shape, where the counters had once stood. At the far side of the room was a recess, which held a large old fashioned deep-freeze cabinet. Scattered over the floor were the remnants of the shop's stock, accurately dating its heyday — 'invisible' hair nets in cellophane packets, tins of boot polish and — could they be? Indeed, they were! 'Blanco'! Little packs of 'Blanco' each with its tiny sponge.

I was immediately transported into my childhood at the sight of those once-familiar boxes. Our summer sandals of white canvas were blanco-ed at bed-time, with the judiciously-wetted sponge. On summer evenings they stood outside, on the kitchen windowsill to dry in the sun. If the weather was wet, which it rarely seemed to be in those halcyon days, the sandals were placed in the hearth to dry overnight and be ready next morning, in all their pristine whiteness, for the walk to school. Woe betide the child who entered the classroom with sandshoes that were not freshly whitened. The teacher's disapproving glare, as she fixed her steely eye on those shoes, immediately labelled the blushing owner as slovenly!

The sight of those boxes had aroused in me feelings of nostalgia and lost in my musings, I gazed round the 'shop' with a half-smile. It was wiped off my face, however, and I came down to earth with a bump, as the depressing dilapidation of the place struck me. Ignoring the floor which was, after all, Cyril's province, I desperately looked for bonus points.

The ceiling was beamed with genuine adzed oak and the alcove containing the freezer had once been a fireplace and had above it what appeared to be a huge oak timber from a mediaeval ship. I consoled myself that a good cleaning and some cosmetic paintwork would work wonders and, certainly, the room had possibilities to someone with our imagination. It was when we entered the last, remaining, downstairs room that the ultimate shock came. At least, we thought it was the final shock, little knowing what lay in store.

It was quite a large room, but had only one tiny window, which allowed little light to seep through the grimy panes. As we peered through the gloom, we could just make out a heap of coal in one corner, and in the middle of the floor, the pale circle of the section through a huge tree trunk. This was evidently a makeshift chopping block, and had a large axe laid across it, with heaps of logs surrounding it.

We looked round in silence, and then saw a sight which would take more thought, work and (worse luck) money to put right than all we had seen, up to now.

Under the window was a shallow stone sink, with a single cold tap above it. From the back of the lead pipe leading to it, spurted a jet of water. This was propelled with such pressure that the water was being forced into the wall.

"Does it need a new washer?" I queried.

"No, love. There's a hole in the pipe," she answered.

"Er — has it been like that long?" Cyril put in.

"Well, it's been like it ever since we've lived here, and that'll be five years," came the reply. "We aren't on the meter and we don't use this back-place, so we've never bothered to do owt about it."

When we went outside, the result of the never-bothering was only too obvious. There was an ominous bulge in the wall, which, in fact, appeared ready to collapse at any moment.

As we trudged and slithered through the neglected orchard, to the stable with its attached, lean-to pig-sty, Paula and I dropped back.

"I could live here," she whispered.

"So could I," I murmured.

I must be mad! What was I saying? Sanity had fled, as my

imagination took over and I envisaged what could be accomplished with hard work. My imagination didn't stretch as far as Cyril's reaction, however. His poker-face gave nothing away, and we'd no idea how he felt about the place.

Upon re-entering the 'back-place,' as the owner had called it, we received yet another nasty shock. Not only was the wall running with dampness and bulging outwards but, upon looking up, we saw daylight leaking through the pantiles. The beams were there, strong and massive, but above, where the ceiling should have rested, was space. The tattered remnants of a ceiling were certainly up there, but that was all.

"What happened up there?" Cyril almost croaked.

Glancing up casually, as one used to the sight, Mrs. Walker replied, "Oh, t'granary floor fell in, about thirty years ago, under a load of barley. Nobody's used it since, so it doesn't matter."

It was in a heavy silence that we followed her round the upstairs, where there were two good-sized bedrooms and, also, a third, which opened, rather strangely, off the bathroom.

What a lot there was to consider! We weighed up the pros and cons during hours of discussion that evening. Though the condition of the property was daunting, we felt that it was now or never and eventually decided to take a chance. Once the first step was taken, it was like setting off on a helter-skelter, at such a pace did events move.

Our own house was put on the market and, to our amazement, sold as soon as it was advertised. Meanwhile, we again set out for 'Rose Dene,' before any other fools could snap up the hovel from under our noses. Mr. Walker was obviously delighted at the speed with which we'd reached a decision, and called his wife.

"Sal, this young man's made an offer. It's a cash deal. What d'you think?"

"I'm game if you are," came the reply; Cyril preening himself at being labelled a young man, suddenly found his hand seized and vigorously pumped up and down, in the age-old sign of a bargain struck. "Done then," said the old man.

"Done," said my husband.

Done? It was less than twenty-four hours since we'd first viewed the property. I suddenly had a feeling of panic. Indeed, of utter and complete panic, at the speed with which events were proceeding.

Although we're on the surface your normal, hum-drum, middle-aged couple, we've always been given to the sudden impulse. This, however, capped the lot, and it was with an uneasy feeling in the pit of my stomach that I trailed after the others, for a second look round. It didn't really seem any worse than I recollected and I stood, looking at the village from the landing window, musing over what needed to be done. Suddenly, I heard Cyril ask.

"What's that?"

Turning I saw a door, which we'd missed yesterday, as it was papered to match the walls.

"Oh, that's just the old attic. You don't want to go up there. It's dark and filthy."

"Yes, I'd like to see it."

"It's only full of old rubbish," she protested.

"I think we'll have a look."

With obvious reluctance, she opened the door, to reveal yet another staircase, winding up into darkness. There were only a couple of glass tiles in the roof and just a few pieces of furniture could be seen. "Old, not antique," I mentally labelled them, and didn't bother to go more than halfway.

On the way home Paula and I discussed our plans for the property; did I "think funds would run to a pony, or even a horse?" she wondered. Eventually, it dawned on us that Cyril hadn't spoken since he'd left the attic.

"What's the matter, love? You're not having second thoughts, are you?" I queried. "It's got such possibilities."

"It's absolutely riddled with woodworm up in that attic," came the gloomy reply.

My heart plummeted bootwards.

"Woodworm?" I repeated, in consternation. Could there be any more body-blows to come? We'd never encountered woodworm before, and had no idea of the cost of dealing with it, nor, in this case, whether it could be dealt with. In our keeness to acquire this not-so desirable property, we'd broken all our own rules. Normally, our offer would have been tendered in writing, containing the magic phrase, 'Subject to contract and survey.'

This time, however, we'd left ourselves no such loophole. Hands had been shaken, signifying a gentleman's agreement which was, both to us and the Walkers, as binding as a written contract.

We felt honour-bound to go ahead with the purchase, but the fact that our own house had sold immediately, with no haggling over price, made it seem all the more desirable. Many a time, in the weeks that followed, I looked round my home and garden and wondered why we were giving it all up to go out 'into the sticks' for what was, in truth, just a whim.

There was one shred of comfort. A survey assured us that, though there was Death Watch Beetle, as well as woodworm, present in the attic, it could be eradicated and, in fact, only needed 'cottage treatment.' Recollecting cathedral appeal funds, I felt quite smug at the thought of Death Watch Beetle (when defunct, of course). It was, to my mind, quite a status symbol, and gave me a feeling of one-upmanship.

Counterbalancing, or even outweighing, this report, came the village builder's news that the wet wall would need to be demolished and rebuilt. We had already made up our minds that the barn would be our kitchen, so arranged to have a large window in the south-facing wall. Ironically, the sale of our house in York went like a dream, whereas the building work at 'Rose Dene' was beset with the predictable, and not-so predictable, hitches. Why do builders suddenly disappear for days at a time?

Eventually moving-day came, and our new kitchen was still wall-less — kitchenless, in fact! Every dog and child in the village seemed to be dodging between the acroprops where our wall was to be and running into the void which we referred to as 'the kitchen.' Security was obviously a feature of town life, and ignored in the country. What was the use of locking the door when the south wall consisted of acroprops curtained by tarpaulin sheets?

Eventually, the inquisitive children drifted away to bed, and we chased out the last of the dogs, mentally resolving that our first purchase must be interwoven fencing, with which to ensure our privacy. Feeling extremely vulnerable, with no kitchen wall, we dragged ourselves upstairs, wondering if we were, indeed, as stupid as our friends and relatives believed. However, the die was cast, and a new life lay before us. Whether better, or worse, than our life in York, it would certainly be different.

CHAPTER THREE

As with all nightmares, this particular one ended and we were, at last, settled into a completed home. Well, that's not quite true but, at least, the kitchen wall was built and the outside of the house coated with paint, so white as to dazzle the eyes.

At a later date, we discovered that our large, kitchen window had given rise to much speculation in the village. Rumours were rife that we were going to open that delight of delights, a fish and chip shop. As the nearest was five miles away, this conjecture probably accounted for much of our apparent popularity. On our part, we congratulated ourselves on choosing such a friendly and pleasant place in which to live. Even when their hopes were dashed, however, the people of Cottingwith were still as friendly and pleasant, so the wisdom of our choice was confirmed.

We'd agreed to buy 'Rose Dene' in February, but didn't move in until May. Although rough and tufty at the beginning of the year, the grass had been reasonably short. Now, however, most of it was waist high and, in fact, in the orchard, the grass and undergrowth almost reached Cyril's chest.

There was a story that, a few years previously, the villagers had over-wintered a group of sea-side donkeys. When they came to be rounded up at Whitsuntide, to return to their seasonal jobs, two were missing. Eventually, believing them to have strayed away, their owner loaded the rest into the horse-boxes, and returned them to their summer quarters. It was not until a fortnight later, when their spring mating-calls led to investigation, that the two strays were found, hidden in the long grass of our orchard. Faced now with the rampant growth, we could well believe the tale.

It was certain that no lawn-mower could tackle the jungle but nothing daunted, Cyril drove into town, in search of a scythe. As we were surrounded by farms whose yards and barns contained combine-harvesters and other huge mechanical puzzles, at whose uses I couldn't even guess (so much had farming changed) I was rather derisive and suggested that he should try the museums or antique shops.

To my surprise, however, he came back bearing in triumph a gleaming, obviously new, positively lethal-looking weapon. I use the word 'weapon' advisedly. The long handle and wickedly-sharp, curved blade conjured up pictures of mediaeval peasants defending their homesteads. I'd never been too keen on this particular venture, but there seemed to be no alternative. Cyril laughed at my fears.

In his youth, the cornfields had been opened for the binder with scythes, and he was confident of his ability to handle the implement. Like swimming or riding a bike, using a scythe was a skill which, once learnt, was never forgotten, he insisted. As my adult attempts at bike-riding are accompanied by wobbles and frequent dismountings, this did nothing to allay my fears. As Cyril strode towards the orchard, looking like a younger version of Father Time, I trailed miserably in his wake. For his sake I put on a brave face but, inside, I was in a state of dithering dread, certain that his lack of practice would result in maiming, if not amputation, of both legs.

While I climbed the fence, for a grandstand view of the impending catastrophe, Cyril made his way to the top corner of the orchard. He took out a sharpening stone and drew it along the curve of the scythe. What was the fool doing? I wondered silently. Surely the blade was razor-sharp already? This ritual over, he looked round, slowly and reflectively. This did nothing for my morale. He was putting off the moment of truth, I told myself. For all his brave words he wasn't really confident. I sat on the fence, my heart in my mouth, as he tried a few tentative sweeps. Suddenly, a grin split his face as he got the feel of the rhythm. As each foot came forward, the great blade curved round, and a swathe of grass fell before it.

It was a timeless, graceful movement. I realised that I'd been holding my breath and, with its release, my fears fled and my pride overwhelmed me. Let the lordly young farmers cover the fields, sitting high on their grinding, snarling juggernauts but, here, with the silence broken only by the rhythmic swish of the blade and the sighing fall of the swathes, was a fulfilment known to generations of our ancestors.

Luckily for us, the weeks that stretched ahead were to throb with heat, under skies of unsullied blue. Each evening was like the beginning of a holiday, as we drove down the winding lane to the village, after our day in the town. This was especially true of Fridays, when there stretched ahead a whole weekend of, what can only be called, hard labour. We were masochists, of course. Nobody in their right minds would voluntarily punish their bodies as we did, over and over again. Looking back, the sheer magnitude of the undertaking was ridiculous, to be tackled by a middle-aged couple

26

The fulfilment of a dream.

and a teenage girl. We never, of course, looked at the project as a whole, otherwise we could never have gone ahead. Each task was tackled as a job on its own, and so we inched our way forward to what was, I think, the fulfilment of a dream.

That sounds rather smug, but we'd undoubtedly built up a picture of what we felt we could achieve and, if we could help it, nothing was going to stop us — apart from complete mental or physical breakdowns, which sometimes seemed imminent!

The house had been labelled as a five-year plan. It was, after all, habitable, though falling very short of our ideal home. The immediate urgency was the cleaning of the land and the planting of soft fruit and vegetables. I did keep reminding Cyril that I also wanted a lawn and a flower-border, but this was way down his list. I don't really know why it was so high on mine. When was I ever going to sit on a lounger? I wondered. The nettles became personal enemies. I have never encountered such nettles! Strong and dark as they massed in groups, anchored into the ground by huge, thick ropes of yellow roots, which seemed to creep along forever. I felt that each lot were waiting to do battle with me, as I donned gloves and went out to the fray. I forked, sifted and scrabbled among the soil, tugging out the tangled masses, but no matter how I battled,

27

there always seemed to be others; they were Triffid-like in tenacity.

We won, of course, in the end. Gradually, after months of physical struggle, during which Cyril lost two stones, we could see the fruition of our plans. The fruit bushes which had stood, higgledy-piggledy, where we had planned our lawn, were dug up and transplanted into regimented rows, for easier picking. This was no mean feat, when overgrown gooseberry bushes had no intention of being prised from their beds. Their wickedly-long thorns clawed at our faces and arms, until we looked as though we'd encountered a wild-cat in an alley. We even had the temerity to transplant four elderly apple trees, which seemed to have escaped from the orchard. Not only that, but they all survived the transplant — so did we!

"I 'ave 'eard," Mrs. Walker had confided when last we saw her, "that there's an aw'd fireplace at t'back of yon wall," nodding towards an outer wall of the 'back-place.' Suckers for a bit of mystery, we'd pricked up our ears at this hint of excitement. We were determined, however, that the land must take priority over the house, otherwise, it would never be tamed into submission. This titillating piece of information, therefore, was pushed to the back of our minds, for future investigation.

Come the autumn, the garden was reasonably mastered, and our thoughts turned to the inside of the house. Deciding to leave the shop/dining-room until later, we determined to concentrate on the kitchen, with the aim of getting it done and usable by Christmas. This target wasn't as easy to achieve as perhaps it sounds. All that had been done up to this point was rebuilding the wall, complete with new window, and the fixing of a rather incongruous-looking sink unit in place of the old stone sink. We were faced with several alternatives for a starting point. Those old, worm-eaten boards which had not succumbed to the weight of the barley, thirty years previously, still formed a jagged fringe across some of the beams. The beams themselves were coated with innumerable applications of a rust-coloured concoction which was later identified as red-rudd. Why do ruddy cheeks sound pleasant? This particular shade was anything but. The floor, of course, was uneven. It was too much to expect anything else and, to complete the picture, one wall, though seemingly sound, was crazed and cracked all over its surface.

"What about that fireplace, then?" Cyril asked, as we looked thoughtfully round. "Do we take a chance and see if there's anything behind this wall?"

28

"Decisions! Decisions!" I mocked, knowing full well that his decision was already reached.

Curiosity vied with apprehension. What if we made a start on the demolition job, only to find that there was nothing behind the wall but fresh air? There was a chimney standing above the level of the kitchen roof, but who was to say whether what should be below it hadn't been knocked down centuries before? The older, back part of the house bore testimony to the whims and fancies of previous owners, in the changes in the pattern of the bricks, where windows and doors had been bricked up and others created.

No planning permission was needed in those days and yet the house had survived. I wonder if the modern breeze-block erections, with their ninety per cent mortgages, will last even one hundred years, much less four hundred? I doubt it.

The one thing in the house's favour when we bought it had been its solidity and now we were contemplating breaching it.

"Thickest walls in t'village, your 'ouse," the shop-keeper had often told us, so, if the end wall was, indeed, an outside one, perhaps we couldn't do much damage.

We moved round the kitchen, tapping the walls. That particular wall certainly resounded rather differently to our taps than the others. We knew from the windows in the other rooms, that the outer walls were about eighteen inches thick and this one certainly didn't sound so solid.

Cyril took the plunge.

"There's a whole weekend before us. Let's stop shilly-shallying and have a go."

So, have a go, we did!

I was for starting at a top, or bottom corner, so that any repairs would be less noticeable if we really damaged the wall.

Cyril, however, is made of sterner stuff. Selecting a hammer and bolster-chisel from his, by now, considerable stock of tools, he attacked the wall in the dead centre. Paula and I craned forward to watch the first blow. To our amazement, a sizeable hole appeared. In fact, Cyril almost fell forward when the strength of his first blow met with so little resistance. We backed off, as we were showered with dust and fragments.

"Good," he grunted, "There is a gap behind. This is only a false wall, of laths and plaster."

Eagerly, we pressed forward, to give him a hand. The partition wall was fairly fragile and, by pulling and tearing at it with our fingers, while Cyril gave a few well-placed swipes with the hammer, we were soon able to enlarge the hole. As soon as the gap was large enough, Cyril exercised his male prerogative and poked his head through.

"Ve-ery interesting," he grinned back at us, teasingly.

"What is?" we demanded, but he refused to satisfy our curiosity.

"Wait and see," was all we got. I felt like seizing his legs and pushing him through but, apart from relieving my feelings, it wouldn't have done any good. Instead, we fell upon the wall, tearing and yanking at it as fast as we could. We were soon engulfed in a cloud of plaster and dust. It coated us completely. It was in our hair, down our nails and up our noses. As the wall came away, we could make out, in the cavity behind, some kind of range, though what type was not yet clear.

"Just a minute," insisted our foreman, as we all sneezed and coughed amid the dust. "Let's take a breather and then get rid of this lot," indicating the pile of debris which surrounded us.

I switched on the kettle in the other kitchen, and we went outside to get some fresh air. I couldn't help laughing, when I took a good look at the others. They looked like black members of the old Minstrel Show. Then I realised that I must be the same. What our lungs were like, I daren't imagine. While we had coffee and breathed fresh air, the dust was settling and we approached our work in a more organised fashion.

We pulled out the laths from the piles of rubbish and these were snapped into convenient lengths for kindling. The plaster and dust were swept up and shovelled into the barrow, which Cyril wheeled outside. Working systematically, it wasn't long before we got rid of the false wall. The outer wall, like all those at the back of the cottage, was, we later discovered, a true mediaeval wall, with its plaster reinforced with horsehair. Our whole attention, however, was at this time directed towards the fireplace.

There had originally been an inglenook and the beam was still in position. Into the cavity had been fitted a Yorkshire range. I expect they have other names in other counties, but that's the name by which we'd always known them. At first, we could make out very little as it was masked by an enormous quantity of soot, spilling from the fireplace, right out over the floor. As we were already filthy, tackling the soot could make little difference, so it was back to

The kitchen range first revealed.

. . . and refurbished.

the shovelling and barrowing once more. Gritting our already gritty teeth, we set to work with a will.

The reward was certainly worth the effort. By the time the weekend's work was over, we were the proud possessors of a little gem of a black, cast-iron range. It was absolutely complete, with an oven at one side of the fireplace and, at the other, a side-boiler for hot water. Across the front, spanning the fireplace, was what is known as a 'reckon.' This is an iron bar furnished with various adjustable hooks to hold skillets and kettles over the fire. Not only did these slide along the reckon, but they could also be raised and lowered acccording to the amount of fuel on the fire beneath.

Everything was intact. There was even an enormous, long-handled ladle for scooping the hot water from the side-boiler.

We'd never seen one so beautifully-preserved, outside a museum. It was our good fortune that the laths had obviously been fixed across the front and the wall plastered, leaving the range as it was last used, with nothing discarded. Even the brass knob was still in place on the oven door. The only missing item was the 'Tidy Betty.' At least that was what our parents had called it, though I believe its real title is an 'ash-pan.' However, Tidy Betty has a better, homelier sound, and that's what it was called.

Again, luck smiled on us. (About time, too, I felt.) On recounting our weekend's discovery to the staff at school, I was offered a Tidy Betty by one of my colleagues. (Yes, that was her name for it, too!) Of course, I jumped at the offer, though I remembered that they varied considerably in size. Upon bringing it home, I found it to be an ideal fit and it completed the range, perfectly. It even bore two brass knobs, smaller editions of the one on the oven door. To add to its charms, the front moulding contained the words: 'Home Sweet Home.'

Not only did the old range give us a lot of pleasure, as we gazed on it with pride, but it was, in fact, a true museum piece. The front of the oven door bore a plate: 'Walkers of York,' by which were were able to date it as being over a hundred years old. A few months after our bringing the range into the world again, we read an article in a newspaper, which featured the firm, 'Walkers of York.' To our delight and pride, it was quite a famous firm, and had made the railings round Peaseholme House in York and, I believe, round the Admiralty in London. In addition to being a source of pride, our old range really worked. During the winter of power cuts, we baked bread, cakes, pastry, and even our own cream-crackers in the oven, while the little fireplace burned all the twigs, logs and broken branches we could gather, in addition to supplying a constant supply of hot water from the side-boiler. Not for the first time since moving to the country were we to wonder if so-called progress really is a forward step.

It's a good thing we weren't paying by the hour for all the work we put into the kitchen. Paula and I spent every evening for two weeks, sitting astride the beams scraping off layers of red ochre, until we, at last, reached bare oak. Cyril, meanwhile, was tackling the uneven floor, grinding and smoothing the surface, ready for tiling. Always, of course, we worked in clouds of what can only be called 'mucky dust.' I often thought of a quotation I'd learned for School Certificate English (that dates me!). The words referred to sand but, in my mind, they were linked inexorably with dust: 'Dust! Dust! Dust! Still dust, and only dust, and dust, and dust again.!'"

At last, our work on the kitchen was over. The old beams were stained dark oak and surrounded by a sparkling white ceiling. The floor was tiled and the crazed wall stripped of its plaster (amid even more dust!) and the exposed brickwork cleaned and sealed. Queening it over all sat the little stove, with a cheerful fire in the grate, reflecting on the beams and walls. We felt a justifiable pride as we looked round. We'd retained all that was worthwhile of the old and yet it combined well with what we'd introduced.

We certainly seemed to have a lucky streak as far as fireplaces were concerned. It was the following year before we felt like tackling the shop. The kitchen was certainly worth the hours of hard slog, not to say both mental and physical exhaustion, which creating it had cost us, and so we decided to see what we could do to transform the old shop into a dining-room.

The first job, Cyril decided, was to remove the peg-board, which lined the freezer recess. Upon beginning to lever it away, we realised that it was a huge, inglenook fireplace, more than eight feet wide. We were once again deluged with a downfall of soot and rubble from the chimney.

"Here we go again," I mentally groaned.

However, as usual, we survived. Once again, looking like defectors from the Black and White Minstrels, we started to shovel and barrow, like the old hands we undoubtedly were. As soon as we'd cleared the floor of the inglenook, we ducked under the supporting beam and stood in the alcove, peering upwards. Although over eight feet wide at the bottom, the chimney tapered, in the space of three storeys, to the chimney-pot, which crowned its summit.

"I'd better sweep it, before we do any more," said Cyril, as flakes of soot with bits of rubble and brick dust rained down on us.

Having started out life on an isolated farm, chimney-sweeping was one of the skills Cyril possessed, together with the brushes to go with it. However, there was no way we could mask off the huge opening, so down the dislodged soot had to come — centuries of it, or so it seemed!

In those first years at 'Rose Dene,' I often caught sight of myself in old jeans and filthy shirt, hair covered with a head-square, and eyes looking out, whitely and wildly from a begrimed face, and wondered what the girls at school would have said if they could have seen me. One of my favourite pieces of advice was, "It'll do, won't do," meaning that if they looked at a garment and thought, "It'll do," it was too grubby to wear. Nowadays, I was rarely anything but grubby, nay, filthy, at weekends.

"All in a good cause," I thought, and set to work on the soot.

Once we could again duck into the ingle and look upwards, we were rather overawed at what we'd done. We couldn't live with the gaping void and all the draughts which would blow down it. Perhaps we'd been fools even to open it up. As we grew used to the gloom in the chimney, Cyril exclaimed:

"Look!"

Following his pointing finger, I saw, mounting up the right side of the chimney, a series of hand and foot-holes.

"Tom, in the 'Water Babies'," said Cyril.

Of course! They had been used by sweeps'-boys to clean the chimney. Although we knew that such chimneys existed, we'd always imagined them in mansions. I'd never thought of them in ordinary houses. Gazing up, I felt a surge of pity for the little lads who'd crawled up that chimney in years gone by; fair enough, we were covered with grime and were breathing the pervading smell of it but, with us, it was from choice, where they'd had neither choice nor any respite from the choking soot, day after day. We did, however, feel excited at yet another touch of history discovered in our home.

Although we were loath to hide the hand and foot-holes, there

34

was no practical way we could leave the chimney open but, exactly what to do with it provoked hours of discussion. We hoped to restore it to its original state, of course, but would like to have it actually in use.

"If I blocked up the chimney, just leaving a gap above the dog-basket, the smoke would still blow down," mused Cyril.

We'd already got enough large, flat stones to pave the floor of the inglenook, and Cyril intended to build a stone-seat at one side. The dog-basket was ordered from a blacksmith but our big problem remained unsolved — how to channel the smoke so that it rose up the chimney, instead of wafting round the room.

We'd thought of a copper canopy, but a look through the price-lists had made us think again.

"Why can't you make one?" I ventured.

"Make what?"

"A copper canopy."

Cyril looked as though he couldn't believe his ears. He'd always suspected that I was daft, but now I'd proved it.

"No!" I protested, at his look of incredulity, "You could, out of an old copper cylinder."

He looked over at Paula and turned his eyes heavenwards.

"She's flipped, at last!"

Many years later, he told me that this was the most shattering suggestion I'd ever made to him. His immediate thought was, "She thinks I can work magic!"

I was unaware of how preposterous the idea seemed to him. I was carried away with enthusiasm and eagerly seized pencil and paper to illustrate what I meant.

"If we could get an old hot water cylinder, you could cut off the top and bottom with tin-snips, and then open it out. We can polish it and then cut out a canopy shape, leaving two side pieces, which, when reversed, could be attached to the front, to make a canopy."

I could see it in my mind's eye, and thought Cyril was being a defeatist, which is unlike him. I'm very good at planning things, but have no conception of any difficulties which may be encountered in the practical development of my plans.

Seeing that I was serious, Cyril studied the sketches. To my disappointment, he made no comment, merely looked thoughtful. However, after lunch, he sauntered casually down the village in the direction of a builder's yard, returning in a few minutes with a

35

The home-made copper canopy.

copper cylinder under one arm. It had been taken out of a house as useless because the seam leaked, and so cost us nothing.

"If it doesn't work," I confided in Paula, "We can bash it with a hammer and put it over a coffee table top."

To Cyril, I gave no hint that I had any doubts; when he set to work with the tin-snips, I drew out templates of the shapes, fitting them together, to show that my idea would really work. Little details as to how to join the three pieces were left to Master-Mind. After all, he was the practical one. I was merely the designer. When the three pieces were cut, we burnished them to a glowing copper colour. This was more easily said than done, beginning, as it did, with wire wool, working through scouring powder and ending with Brasso — all applied with plenty of elbow-grease, by all three of us. At last we were satisfied with the gleam, and, armed with an electric drill, hammer and a paper bag which contained copper rivets, Cyril went outside, motioning us to bring the canopy pieces.

Was there no end to his ingenuity? I wondered, as he placed a four-stone weight firmly on to a tree stump, to act as a make-shift anvil. I'd known all along that he wouldn't fail me. I've often thought that if I had to endure a shipwreck, live on a desert island or go on a wagon train, Cyril is the companion I'd choose. This isn't just because he's my husband, but because if something is humanly possible, he can usually do it.

When our children were small, if anything went wrong or any toy was broken, they were always assured by me, "Daddy will put it right."

It was years before he told me what a feeling of responsibility this placed upon him, but I always had implicit trust in his ability to cope, and here I was, proved right again. When he came back to the house, carrying what can only be described as a magnificent specimen of a copper canopy, I could only gasp. It was far better than I'd ever imagined. I don't know to this day how it was actually fixed on the back wall of the inglenook, but fixed it was, to become the focal point of the loveliest room in the house. One of my cosiest memories of our life at 'Rose Dene' is of sitting in the inglenook, roasting chestnuts over the fire.

CHAPTER FOUR

For quite a time, I had eyed speculatively the one or two goats which were tethered by the roadside on the way into York. They had consumed a prodigious amount between our morning and evening journeys. It was some time before I broached the idea that had been simmering in my mind.

"Have you thought of a goat?"

"A goat?" with a look of astonishment. "Certainly not! They're as daft as sheep."

Cyril was a pig man.

He quite liked cows, tolerated horses, but despised sheep. To him, sheep were the essence of stupidity and, probably as a relic of his Sunday-School days, sheep and goats were indivisibly linked in his view. I soon noticed, however, that he too, began to eye the roadside goats with a degree of interest.

Our trouble was that we had rather too much grass. If he tried to keep the orchard and lawns under control, Cyril couldn't keep up with the rest of the work in the chapel garth, which was the small field devoted to vegetables and soft fruit. Not only was the hoeing and weeding a constant job but, once the fruits of our labours were ripe, we were kept busy, dealing with enormous quantities of produce. We picked, blanched and froze — jellied, jammed and preserved. Later, there were apples and pears to gather, sort and store, as well as gallons of wine and cider to make and bottle. Although our normal labours never ceased, from July to October life was a hectic round of harvesting and I often wondered how our evenings had been spent before we opted for the good life.

Now, we came home after our day's work to face three or four hours dealing with whatever glut we had at that particular time. I think the only really unpleasant thing was the foul smell of blanching cauliflower. As I saw Cyril approaching the kitchen with yet another tin bath of caulis when I had every worktop covered with plastic bags full and the air was full of the nauseating pong, the only thing which kept me from screaming was the thought of a winter of plenty. The busier we became, the more often I pictured a pretty little goat, munching its way across the orchard like a self-propelled Hoover, saving Cyril a lot of work. Perhaps, though, details of this were a bit vague in my daydream; we may even have the added bonus of goat's milk. We have neither of us had much experience of goats but, after all, one animal is very much like another, or so I kidded myself.

Although I'd planted the seed in Cyril's mind, it came to fruition before I'd expected.

"In-kid nanny for sale. Good milker. £10."

The advert seemed to leap out of the page at me. The 'phone number was in the next village. Surely it was aimed specifically at us.

"Shall I ring?" I nagged several times. Each time I received the response of the true bargainer.

"Not yet; let him simmer."

Not for nothing was he the grandson of a horse-dealer! I could see this treasure slipping from our grasp. Ten pounds was a low enough asking price. Surely she'd soon be snapped up. In the end, my pleading met with grudging consent and I dashed to the 'phone. Not only was she still for sale, but the owner offered to bring her over for viewing. As we had no trailer, this solved the problem of transport if we decided to buy her. We recognised the deviousness of this offer. It would be more difficult to decide not to buy if she were actually on our property. However, we prided ourselves that we were more than a match for any trader, if we decided against the purchase. That, of course, was before we'd met the goat.

About half-an-hour later, they arrived at the back door. He was a seedy-looking character, with the crafty face and shifty eyes of a man who's out to make a quick buck, no matter how. Drooping dejectedly behind him at the end of a chain was the mangiest, most miserable-looking creature one could meet.

I recognised her immediately, as the only grotty goat we saw on our daily journeys — a far cry from the dainty creature I'd hoped for. While other, younger goats looked spruce and white, her off-grey coat hung dull, lifeless and tufty. What she really resembled, to my disappointment, was an old, moulting goatskin rug, tossed carelessly over the frame of one of those bikes with cow-horn handle-bars. Every rib stood out. Her hip-bones stood up sharply from her frame. As she shifted her weight from one foot to the other, we could see the neglected hooves curling under, digging into her feet. Her whole attitude was one of hopelessness, which immediately struck a chord of pity in me. She may not be what I'd expected, but there was no way I was going to allow her to go back with that man. If ever an animal mirrored ill-treatment, she undoubtedly did.

I didn't speak. Throughout many years, we've built up a pattern of bartering, and Cyril always makes the first move.

"How old is she?" moving round to inspect her from all angles.

"Nine," came the quick response.

Nine? If he'd said ninety, I wouldn't have been surprised. Contemplating her lethal-looking horns, I wondered if they bore annual-rings. Her jaws moved rhythmically and I caught a glimpse of huge, elongated yellow teeth. She must be more than nine. I was sure that I'd once read that domestic nannies lived to about twenty years. I silently prayed that Cyril would buy her. I longed to give her a good home.

He bent and lifted one of the poor, tortured feet.

"These are in a mess!" he accused.

"Well, they are ready for trimming. I'll grant you that."

Cyril glowered, as though ready to knock him down.

"I'll give you eight."

"Nine."

"Eight-and-a-half is as far as I'll go."

"Done!"

The goat raised her head and gave me an appraising look from her tawny eyes. I'd never known before that goats had oblong pupils. It gives them quite a satanic look; strange, unearthly. My eyes fell before her gaze.

Once paid, he was ready for off, presumably before we changed our minds.

"What's her name?" I called, as he darted through the gate.

"Tinkerbell," he threw over his shoulder.

If ever a name was wrongly-bestowed, it was that one.

"Tinkerbell?" Anything less fairylike it was hard to imagine. Nevertheless, the die was cast, and Tinkerbell was ours, for good or ill.

I'd never been close to a goat before, and had always understood that the smell was, to say the least, obnoxious. What faint odour arose from her was, however, quite pleasant. She smelt of new-mown hay as do, I always think, elephants and other herbivores. We eyed her a trifle uneasily. Her horns were exceedingly large, and we'd no idea what her temper was like. Her previous owner had assured us that his children played with her, but she looked, to our eyes, to have very little play left in her. Carefully, Cyril picked up her chain and gave it a slight tug. Obediently, she followed him to the stable where he gave her a good meal and bedded her down for the night. From the way she gingerly placed her feet, it was obvious that each step caused her pain, but we decided to wait until morning to tackle anything further. Cyril was fairly confident that he could ease her, so we left her in warm, clean bedding until the next day.

Looking back, it was surprising how quickly her appearance improved. She never, of course, became a pretty goat. Like many humans, she'd obviously been plain, or even ugly, all her life. She responded however, to thorough brushing, which removed the loose hair and brought a gloss, albeit a dull one, to her coat. The first job, of course, was to relieve her feet.

Although until now she had seemed docile enough, the pedicure was approached with a certain trepidation. When her chain was thoroughly secured, and I was firmly holding her collar, Cyril tackled her feet, eyeing her rather warily. Selecting and discarding instruments, scissors, secateurs and files, he eventually settled on wire-cutters for the operation.

While I held on to the collar and stroked her soothingly, he trimmed and pared each hoof until it was back to normal. We then bathed her feet in an antiseptic lotion and, though freedom from pain wasn't instantaneous, she obviously felt much better. Days of browsing in the lush grass of the orchard, plus an additional ration of rolled oats and linseed cake in the evening, brought about such a transformation that, within a few weeks, her previous owner would not have recognised her. I even rubbed "Olive Oil" into the dry horns to raise a shine on them.

Unlike Androcles and the lion, our ministrations didn't strike a chord of gratitude in response. I don't know whether the goat-sign is Capricorn because they are capricious, or whether they're capricious because their sign is Capricorn. Perhaps capricious isn't exactly the right word for Tinkerbell. She wasn't really unpredictable; rather, what the Americans would call, 'just plain ornery.' She spent twenty-four hours of every day plotting and scheming as to how she could outwit us and get to the rose bushes which were her favourite delicacy. No matter how she was tethered, more often than not, she managed at least one escape a day — sometimes several. Houdini would have been a far more appropriate name for her than Tinkerbell.

Contrary to what many people think, goats really do need to be tethered. One reason is that they are browsers rather than grazers,

Tinkerbell planning an escape.

and will raze to the ground any bush they encounter, even the prickliest. Though, when they nuzzle, their lips are as soft as a human kiss, they munch their way steadily through nettles, thistles, and even gooseberry bushes, with no apparent pain, indeed, with obvious relish. The other reason for tethering goats is that, contrary to general opinion, they are fastidious feeders and, far from eating 'anything,' as many people think, they dislike to even eat grass on which they've trodden. If given free rein in the orchard, Tinkerbell would not only have 'barked' all the trees, nibbling it off and so killing them, but she would have refused to eat the grass which she'd trampled down, and wasted. By moving the post and giving her fresh pasture daily, the orchard was cropped and her appetite assuaged.

So, tethered she was, but this daily routine became a battle of wits between her and Cyril. Each morning, he would choose the place to put the stake, with plenty of long grass and perhaps a few wild brambles within her reach. Then, swinging the fourteen-pound hammer, he would bash the stake into the ground. When I say 'stake,' don't get me wrong. This was no ordinary run-of-the-mill stake which would hold a Dobermann Pinscher, or a Bull Mastiff. This was a huge piece of iron, three-and-a-half feet long with a point at one end and a knob at the other — rather like a giant nail. However, no matter how firmly it was hammered in, it was rarely a match for Tinkerbell.

When led out from the stable, she would eye the stake impassively

42

with those amber eyes, lift her lip sardonically and watch him return to the house. All the time, of course, she was considering her strategies, and deciding which ploy to try today. She had two main alternatives, depending on the depth and firmness of the stake, although until we watched carefully, she appeared to free herself by magic.

She would, at first, test the firmness of the ground into which the stake had been hammered. Going up close to the stake, she would set herself four-square before it, lower her head and place her forehead, at the base of her horns, against the top of the stake. Then she would exert pressure. If the stake gave way, she would increase the pressure or even, on occasion, use a rocking movement to loosen it. Once it was loose enough for her purpose, she'd turn round, charge to the full length of her chain, yank the stake from the ground, and off she'd go.

If the stake was too firmly-implanted and this method 'didn't work, she had another, even more ingenious, 'modus operandi.' Going almost to the end of her chain, she would execute a series of leaps, each accompanied by a flick of the neck. This was designed to slide the ring up and, when it reached the highest point, the jerk of the neck whipped the ring off the retaining stake and Tinkerbell had once more achieved her aim.

She would set off, at a brisk trot, for whatever took her fancy as a titillating alternative to boring old grass; be it vegetables, raspberry canes or, delight of delight, roses; stopping, of course, on the way, to nibble the odd flower or try a tasty shrub. This, however, was where she came unstuck. No matter how quietly she tried to sneak off, like Marley's ghost her progress was accompanied by the clanking of chains. Rope won't hold goats, no matter how thick it is. They merely chew through it and walk away. So, although Tinkerbell freed herself with great regularity, there was no way she could divest herself of the tell-tale chain.

Not long after she joined the family, Cyril had been made redundant, so he was usually within earshot when she set out on her foraging expeditions. It's no use chasing runaway animals; they only run away more quickly. The secret is to approach them nonchalantly, as though recapture is the last thing in your mind. Then, when they're within reach, you make your swoop. This is in theory, of course. In practice, it doesn't always work, especially when dealing with an animal of Tinkerbell's calibre.

43

Upon hearing the chain, Cyril would dash from the house, or workshop, spot his prey, and then slow down to, what he hoped was, a casual pace, approaching her by a roundabout route. She would continue to munch away at her chosen titbit, apparently oblivious to his tactics. It was the age-old game of cat and mouse, though which was which I was never sure. Sometimes, it was possible for him to see the direction of the chain and grab the end of it before she realised. If this occurred, she accepted defeat graciously and followed him back to the orchard to be secured more firmly.

More often than not, however, she was just one jump ahead of him mentally, and, as he lunged forward, she would skitter away and eye him disdainfully, from a few yards further on. Cyril would pick himself up and begin the whole business once more. It was humiliating to be outwitted and out-manoeuvred by a goat, but patience was the only answer. If, as sometimes happened, he threw caution to the winds and gave chase, the results were disastrous. She would charge wildly through the crops, her hooves and chain or, worse still, the stake also, flattening and ruining far more than she would have eaten. So patient stalking was the only answer. In the end, he always triumphed and led her back to the orchard, no matter how long it took. Or did she give in, having proved she could do it? We'll never know.

When we'd bought her, she was, of course, in-kid, and it became obvious that her time was drawing near. She rounded out in a matronly way and her udder, which had, until now, been a long skinny bag hanging beneath her, began to fill up. At last, one bright spring afternoon, I received a 'phone call at School. Beaming all over her face, the secretary appeared at my classroom door.

"Mr. Sunley's just rung. Twin girls, all three doing well."

A ripple of excitement ran round the class.

"Was 'Miss' a granny? Of twins?"

I explained that the mother was a goat with nanny kids, which excited my pupils even more. I settled them down to work, with promise of future photographs, but I myself couldn't concentrate. We knew that goats usually do have twins, but for both kids to be nannies was a bonus.

When he picked me up at home-time, Cyril wasn't as jubilant as I'd expected. I fired questions at him all the way home.

"Were there any complications?"

"No."

44

Tinkerbell, without her bra.

"What are the kids like?"
"One cream and one white."
"Are they pretty?"
"Yes."
"What's wrong then?" I burst out at last.
We were, by now, pulling into the drive.
"We-ell, there is a bit of a problem," he confessed. "It's her udder, you see."

See I did, as soon as I opened the gate. Her udder hung, gross and bloated, beneath her, until it actually touched the ground.

Poor Tinkerbell — she certainly wasn't one of nature's winners! I could appreciate Cyril's concern. It wasn't merely the appearance of the thing, which was grotesque — nay, positively indecent — but she must have been in discomfort, or even pain, with it trailing on the ground as she moved.

I studied the poor old lass, trying to see some way of alleviating her pain. Then the full impact of the problem struck me. With no room to reach her teats, Tinkerbell could neither be milked, nor could the kids suckle. The poor little things nuzzled up to her, trying to find the teats but, as these were at ground level, their search was in vain. Our pleasure in the pretty little creatures was marred by the unexpected problem, the like of which we'd never encountered before. How could they be reared, without their mother's milk? Anxiously, Cyril lifted the udder, while I held each kid in turn and

45

tried to place a teat in her mouth, but it was no use. They were still timid and merely struggled in my arms as I tried to persuade them to feed, in this unnatural position.

Things were now getting to a desperate state. Without colostrum, the fluid produced by mammals before the milk comes, they could not survive. We later discovered, in an old book, a recipe for home-made colostrum, using milk, eggs, glucose and codliver oil. At this time, however, we knew of no substitute for that produced by the mother and we knew that this was vital in the first hour or two of the newborn kids' lives.

"Slip across the road and borrow a lamb teat from Fred," said Cyril, as he began to wash out a lemonade bottle.

When I got back with the teat, he was almost lying down to reach Tinkerbell's, and was managing to gently squeeze the life-giving liquid into a small bowl. No way was he able to fit our spanking new milking bucket under her. At last he obtained what we thought to be sufficient for this vital first feed, and quickly transferred it to a warm bottle, to keep it at the right temperature. Sometimes, newly-born animals can be incredibly slow in learning to suck. It should be a natural reaction, but often isn't. However, Coffee and Cream, as we called them, took to the bottle with no difficulty, so this was the first hurdle surmounted.

By now, Tinkerbell had set up a melancholy bleating, and when we examined her, we could see the cause. She had a nasty tear in her udder, where it had caught a piece of thorn as it trailed over the ground. We cleaned and gently bathed it, but couldn't think how to keep it covered, or prevent the same thing from happening again, and again.

"I'll have a go at milking her out and relieving the weight," said Cyril. This was easier said than done, but she seemed to be anxious to co-operate in anything which would relieve her distress. I was rather surprised when Cyril went and fetched an old milking stool! I really couldn't see how he could achieve any success sitting down to milk that pendulous bag. Plonking it down behind Tinkerbell, he seized her back legs and lifted them on to it, so that she was standing at an angle — back legs raised off the ground and udder raised to a more manageable height. Although she looked round at him, in obvious amazement, she obligingly stood as I held her collar and Cyril prostrated himself once more, milking her into a basin. When she was milked dry, he took her and the kids into the stable, while I

46

put the colostrum in the fridge, to be warmed to blood heat later that night, for a second bottle-feed.

"I don't know what we can do about her bag," he said on his return to the house. "I can't see how we can avoid it getting torn and scratched, and there's no way we can keep it free from infection then."

"It's a pity nobody makes goat bra's!" I commented.

Our eyes met.

"Is it possible?" asked Cyril.

I thought for a few minutes.

"I don't see why not."

I went up to my remnant box on the landing, to look for a piece of material big enough and not too garish. Although nobody but us (and the goats) would see it, I felt it would offend her dignity to put her into something flowered, or jazzy. I found a piece of strong, plain brown cotton, which I thought would be suitable and, as I laid it out on the kitchen table, Cyril went out with my tape-measure to take some rough measurements.

The resultant creation may not have been "haute couture," but it braced up Tinkerbell's drooping bosom and prevented cuts and scratches to this delicate area. There were two holes underneath for her teats, and the bra fastened on her back with laces, so that she couldn't reach round and chew it off. It was removed for milking, and she showed no objection to wearing it in between milkings, so, although it looked rather odd, it certainly worked.

We decided, however, that Tinkerbell would bear no more kids. She was obviously a very old lady and had earned her rest. She lived out the rest of her days with us and, although we hadn't expected it, she came into milk each spring, without having kidded, and gave us milk until autumn, for the rest of her life. We gradually built up quite a large herd of goats, but Tinkerbell stands out for sheer guile and cussedness. Even so, she always retained a special place in our hearts. She continued to wind Cyril up with her tricks, right up to the day he went in to find that she'd died peacefully in her sleep, presumably of old age. Though she'd led us some dances, we comforted ourselves that her years with us had been, perhaps, the best of her life, and we thought she'd respected us, as we'd respected her undoubted intelligence.

CHAPTER FIVE

We hadn't been long at 'Rose Dene,' when a nearby farmer offered us the choice of a litter of kittens.

"You'd better go along and choose one — a Tom," I said to Paula and Martin.

Off they went to make their choice. When they came back, Paula was carrying a little ginger tom. Ginger is, perhaps, too harsh a description of his colour. He was a glorious, deep marmalade shade, with a creamy chest. His wide blue eyes stared disdainfully round at us as Paula held him out for our inspection.

"Don't put him down yet," I suggested, "until I've buttered his paws."

"What on earth's that for?" enquired Martin.

"It's always done," I protested. "It stops cats from running away."

When I'd lubricated his paws liberally with butter, he gazed at me and then, slowly and methodically, cleaned each foot in turn.

"He looks so superior, I think we'll call him Sultan," I suggested, while I bustled off to fetch a saucer of milk.

As I placed it on the floor, Paula gently stood him down beside it. No sooner had his feet touched the ground, than he shot off, like a greyhound out of a trap. While we stood aghast, the ginger streak darted across the floor and straight into the fireplace.

"Grab him!" Too late.

Luckily for him, there was no fire in the grate. He paused only for an instant and then, as we made a concerted lunge across the kitchen, he shot up the chimney with what seemed to be the speed of a space-craft from its launching pad.

"He's gone!"

"Can he get right up?"

"How can we get him down?"

The questions were flung thick and fast, as we rushed to peer up the chimney.

Although they were bigger than I was, I elbowed my offspring out of the way and exercised the right of seniority to be the first to try to spot him. I stood in the hearth and poked my head into the chimney opening, twisting to look upwards.

"There he is," I breathed.

He was crouching on a ledge, about a yard and a half up from the fireplace. As I craned upwards, he retreated, growling and spitting down at me, while the blue eyes glowered fiercely from the soot-begrimed face.

In vain we called up, trying to entice him down.

"Here, Puss, Puss!"

"Che-che-che! Here, boy!"

To no avail. The only response our entreaties evoked was an occasional hiss and spit. At the rear of the grate was a ledge where the slack, or coaldust, used to be piled, to be raked as needed on to a glowing fire. Here Paula hopefully placed a saucer of milk, while I went to rummage in the freezer!

Finding a piece of fish, I put it on to boil not only to thaw it, but in order to increase the smell, hoping that, as it wafted up the chimney, it would prove irresistible to Sultan.

Neither of the baited saucers seemed to be of the slightest interest to the kitten, so we left him to his own, rather sooty, devices, carefully closing the kitchen door behind us.

"Wait till Dad comes home. He'll get him down," I promised confidently. As usual, I was convinced that Cyril could solve our problem, and would find some way to rescue the kitten. I suppose that all our heroes have, at some time, feet of clay, and this was the day that my hero showed his. Stripping off his shirt, he stood in the hearth and groped, rather ineffectually, I considered, up the chimney.

"It's no good. I can't reach him," he said, and, in the next breath, "Is tea ready?"

I did feel that this was a somewhat callous attitude, and that he was getting his priorities rather wrong.

"Shall I ring the fire brigade?" I suggested.

The look I got in reply was withering, so say the least. It was obvious that my intelligence had slumped somewhat in my loved one's estimation.

"The fire brigade?" he echoed. "Bring them twelve miles, for a kitten in a chimney? Have you any idea what they'd charge?"

I hadn't even known that they could charge. In my ignorance, I'd believed them to be a sort of poor man's knight errant, to be called upon in life's crises, to rescue cats from chimneys, toddlers from trees and old ladies from lavatories. However, I was wrong, it seemed, and there was nothing to do but wait.

"He'll come down when he's hungry," asserted Cyril, confidently. "Just see that the kitchen doors aren't left open."

Despite several trips to peer up the chimney, the situation remained in stalemate. That evening, when bedtime came, the latest addition to the family was still sitting in solitary state on his ledge.

Come the morning, the two saucers were empty; the fish and milk had been consumed, but Sultan was back on his gloomy perch. As I refilled the dishes, Cyril remonstrated. "He'll have to be starved into coming down. If you feed him there, he'll never come down."

No matter how I hardened my heart during the day, in the evening I filled up the saucers and left them like a votive offering, on the fireback. Each night, I replenished the saucers. Each morning, they were empty and Sultan had withdrawn once more to his retreat. Day after day, after day, this continued. Although, at intervals, I talked up the chimney, wheedling and cajoling, it was to no avail.

At last, after eight days, I reluctantly acceded to Cyril's advice and went to bed, leaving the bowls empty. After all, he'd had regular meals since taking up his position in the chimney, so one night without food wouldn't cause his demise. Next morning I refilled the dishes and placed them in the hearth, inside the fender, but as far away from the grate as possible. I went about my chores as quietly as I could, glancing from time to time towards the fireplace. Eventually, I heard him scrambling in the chimney, so I applied myself to the potatoes I was scraping, trying to assess his progress, though keeping my back turned. At last, I risked a glance. There he was, crouched over the milk, his little pink tongue darting in and out, lapping it up. What an object he looked! The beautiful coat was grimy with soot, and the hearth was covered with black paw prints. Holding my breath, I turned round carefully and, talking soothingly, I approached him. He watched me warily, but remained crouched by the saucers.

"Come on, boy," I whispered, my hand outstretched. "Here, Puss. Here, Sultan."

Reaching out, I rubbed beneath his ears, and caressed under his chin. Slowly, he relaxed and began to purr. Had I won? I stretched out and gathered him to me, soot and all.

From then on, Sultan settled down with me. Though not a productive member of our animal fraternity, he certainly had his uses. As he grew older, his farm-cat ancestry took over, and he became a prodigious hunter, both of mice and rats, keeping the

Sultan was a people's cat.

buildings as clear of vermin as possible. He developed into a fine specimen of cat-hood, and seemed conscious of his beautiful colouring, deliberately seeking out seats which would tone with, or complement, it. The stone seat in the inglenook was furnished with a large cushion of almost the same colour as Sultan's coat, and he spent many hours curled up there, either for reasons of camouflage, or to display his beauty.

Another peculiarity, which I've never known in any other cat, was a love of marmalade. He would sit by the breakfast table, a look of hopeful expectancy on his face, as he gazed wistfully from one to the other. Eventually, his patience was rewarded, and one of us would toss him a piece of toast and marmalade, which he would catch in his mouth and devour with obvious relish. It was clear that it was the marmalade which was regarded as a prize delicacy. We tried him with toast and jam, toast and cheese, or toast and nothing. There was no doubt that the marmalade won, hands down.

Most cats are self-contained, rather disdainful of their owners, and only deigning to allow them ownership on their own terms. Sultan, however was a people's cat, making it obvious that he belonged to us, not to the house. If we sat down, he sat on us. If we went for a walk, he followed us. If we weren't available, he made do with the next best thing, and snuggled up to Hedda, our Alsatian bitch. He seemed to have an abundance of affection, all of which was lavished on us.

When Sultan was about a year old, we rather apprehensively accepted a scrawny little black kitten, for whom there was only one possible name: Lucifer. We needn't have worried about his acceptance of the newcomer. He and Hedda immediately adopted the tiny scrap, like foster parents. It was Sultan, in fact, with a maternal-like patience which warred with his own obvious masculinity, who taught Lucifer to hunt.

When working outside, we would watch in fascination the tip of Sultan's tail twitching through the long grass, hunting for field-mice. When he pounced, he would come back with the poor creature, rigid with terror, held carefully in his mouth. Going up to Lucifer, he would place the mouse carefully before the kitten, and then step back to see how Junior responded. More often than not, at the beginning of the course of tuition, Lucifer's reaction was one of puzzled amazement. He would stare at the luckless mouse with curiosity, then nothing more. The poor little creature would recover his wits and try to escape, only to be the target of a lightning swoop by Sultan, who would present it to Lucifer again and yet again.

"I feel we should stop them," I'd often say.

Cyril, however, always won the day.

"Nonsense! Cats will always hunt. It's their nature."

Certainly, Sultan did his best to instil this into Lucifer. Day after day, he concentrated on the kitten's education in a way we'd never seen before. Perhaps he succeeded too well. Poor little Lucifer never lived to adulthood. He succumbed to a rat-bite when he was only half-grown. Perhaps if he hadn't had such a good tutor, he'd never have tackled a fully-grown rat.

After Lucifer's death, Sultan took to bringing his trophies, luckily defunct, home to us. Most mornings, there was a dead mouse on the back doorstep, and he would sometimes present one or two during the day.

The day was to come, however, when Sultan's hunting instinct was to rouse our displeasure, to put it mildly.

With his redundancy pay, Cyril had invested in some woodworking machinery, and we had opened a little craft shop in the dining room. As an added attraction for customers, we had a large aviary, full of golden, silver, and other fancy pheasants. Lured, as usual, by the 'Livestock' column in the local paper, we decided to

52

invest in a pair of peafowl. We've always been suckers for any form of animal life, and rather fancied a peacock (accompanied, of course, by his rather drab mate) strutting around the garden. Tempting though we found this picture, we realised that, until they became used to us, they would have to be confined, and we already had the ideal place, in our opinion. This was what my family, with teasing affection, referred to as 'Dingley Dell.'

When we had first bought 'Rose Dene,' we obtained some silver birch saplings, which, together with some old blackcurrant bushes and shrubs thrown out by my aunt, we had planted to form a little copse, by the side of the chapel. This was just the right size, and would provide an interesting environment for the birds. Consequently, Cyril spent the rest of the week fencing off Dingley Dell, with six-foot high wire netting. We weren't too sure about their flying ability, though I'd often seen peafowl fly out of the Museum Gardens in York, to beg along the bus queues.

"Perhaps we'd better have something to stop them flying over the top," suggested Cyril. I could see the cost escalating until it cost more to house them than to buy the birds. My sinking heart was raised up again, however, when he explained his plan. It was to drape fine, black nylon strawberry netting from tree-top to tree-top. Although there wouldn't be a complete coverage, we hoped to fool them into not testing it. This was not as easy to accomplish as Cyril had made it sound.

"Will you give me a hand with this?" he asked, in a deceptively casual voice. Having just put the dinner on, I went out for what I anticipated being a few minutes.

I should have known! Where my husband is concerned, very few things are ever straightforward.

This particular exercise involved two pairs of step-ladders, scissors, shears and, later, disinfectant and numerous plasters. Rather than the 'minute' I was asked to spare, it took the best part of two days. In theory, it had seemed so simple.

In practice, it was complicated, time-consuming, and physically exhausting.

Up and down the steps we clambered, heaving, twitching and casting the net over the tree tops and from one to the other. Could these tall and graceful trees have matured, unnoticed, from the saplings which we'd brought on the car roof-rack only a few years ago?

Times without number did one of us begin to mount our steps, only to be catapulted into a bush, as they tipped over on uneven ground. I began to feel that, if it happened just once more, I'd scream and be blowed what the neighbours thought! I could see the funny side, of course, when Cyril shot off, landing in a blackcurrant bush — as long as he didn't land too heavily. For my part, however, I was one of the weaker sex, though you'd never guess, from the jobs I was asked to do, and I was getting fed-up. At last it was all finished, and Cyril went to collect the new residents of Dingley Dell.

I've already said that I suspected that the people of the village thought we were eccentric, to say the least. Our capers in Dingley Dell had roused much speculation as to what we were going to do next, and when Cyril arrived home, it was amazing how many of our neighbours passed, "On my way to the shop!"

There was a buzz of excitement when he lifted from the back of the car, two sacks, each fastened round the neck of a bird, with the exotic, crested heads sticking out.

Were we starting a zoo? In their eyes, we were daft enough. When Cyril had carried them through the gate and released them in Dingley Dell, an old neighbour called round.

"What's yon big blue bod?" he wanted to know. On being told, he showed absolute amazement. "A peacock? Aa's nivver seen yan o' them afore!" he commented, and came through to examine it more closely. "By, 'e's a smasher!" he exclaimed, and so we thought too. He was fully-grown, with a magnificent tail, and his colouring was superb.

The pair settled down well, but remained very shy. The hen, in particular, spent most of her time hiding in the bushes. The cock, for his part, was rather less timid, and we found, by trial and error, that when fed peanuts, he would raise his tail in display, and rattle the feathers. It can't be the reason for their name, but peanuts were certainly a favourite food, and useful when we had visitors to whom we wanted him to show off.

Just after Christmas, we woke to find there had been a very heavy fall of snow, overnight. Cyril thought nothing of it, except to wrap up warmer, when he went out to feed the stock. As he approached Dingley Dell, however, catastrophe met his gaze. The weight of the snow on the netting canopy had dragged it down, until most of it was at ground level. The gaps in the net were now obvious, and though the hen hadn't ventured out, the cock was nowhere to be seen. I was at the window, washing up the breakfast pots, when Cyril came running across the garden.

"What's wrong?" as I went to the door.

"The peacock's escaped!" he called, "Come and give me a hand!"

I put on my coat and, as I ran to the door, I grabbed a towel, with the vague idea that it might provide a blindfold for the bird.

Luckily, the tracks were clear in the freshly-fallen snow, and we'd no difficulty in following him. We only hoped that his escape was fairly recent, and he hadn't time to get far.

"There he is," panted Cyril.

Sure enough, he wasn't far ahead, his beautiful blue colouring showing up vividly against the snow.

From now on, our campaign was conducted in silence, with Cyril motioning in sign language, when and where to go. We didn't know whether or not the peacock could fly, but he hadn't attempted it as yet, otherwise we'd have been sunk. As we converged on him, from two sides, trying to trap him in the corner of a wall, his head darted this way and that, trying to keep us both in view. I was praying that he wouldn't take wing and fly over the wall, while we crept closer and closer to him.

"Now!" hissed Cyril.

As I dived towards him, I tossed the towel over his head, so that, for a moment, he couldn't see, and Cyril grabbed him triumphantly. Deftly, he folded the bird's wings and tucked him under his arm, and we trudged back to restore him to his spouse. The glow of the chase rapidly subsided, as we moved among the bushes, shaking the snow from the netting, and propping it up, as best we could, to act as a makeshift cage.

We never did find out whether our peacock possessed the power of flight. He hadn't tried it to preserve his freedom, and he never tried it when the netting cover was far from complete. After his one adventure, he settled down, quietly, until spring and its attendant mating season arrived.

I was later to recall an occasion when the respectful hush of York library was split by the call of a peacock who was perched on one of the outside windowsills. For a split second, I wondered what the appalling noise could be, as an old lady nearby had dropped her books with the shock, but the incident had receded into the corner of my mind, long before we bought our proud pair.

With the spring, however, this memory was recalled to my mind only too clearly. I was awakened from sleep one morning by the most deafening and terrifyingly raucous screech. I lay for a few moments, wondering what on earth was happening. I thought, at first, that it must be the braying of a donkey. Going to the window and drawing back the curtain, I peeked out. There was nothing in the street to account for the ear-splitting din. Then I saw the bedroom curtains opposite twitch and Betty peered round them. While my gaze was fixed on the village street, hers crossed it and was looking into Dingley Dell.

Suddenly, I recognised the sound, and my heart sank. It was the call of the peacock, ringing out to warn off any who trespassed on his territory. As the nearest rivals were about nine miles away, as the crow, or peacock, flies, it was a useless exercise on his part, but how was he to know it?

After his first few tentative brays, he became more confident, or more aggressive, and his subsequent calls mounted, decibel by decibel. By now, I was in a state of panic. Cyril slept on, oblivious to the noise but there couldn't be many in the village who were such sound sleepers. Our name would undoubtedly be mud. Scrambling

Two little pea-fowl chicks.

56

into dressing-gown and slippers, I ran downstairs in what was to become a regular morning ritual. Looking wildly round the kitchen for inspiration, I grabbed half-a-loaf of bread and, thanking my lucky stars that the morning was dry and mild, headed for the peacock's enclosure.

Luckily for me, his curiosity overcame his passion, and the hunks of bread, thrown through the wire-netting, had the effect of quietening him.

For the next month, the dawn chorus rang out earlier and earlier. I began to leave the diurnal offering ready the night before, and trained myself — or he trained me! — to wake at his first call. Like a sprinter off the block, I was up and out in a flash, curtailing the number of times he gave voice, as I became speedier. Although Betty-over-the-road was kind about it and assured me that her husband wasn't disturbed, I knew that she was and I felt appropriately guilty.

I began to avoid other people in the village, dreading their complaints. None came, however, and I decided they were either heavy sleepers or didn't know the cause of the noise. It seemed worth the disturbance and worry when Cyril came in one day to say that the peahen had made a nest deep in the bushes, and had laid two eggs.

At last, the eggs hatched, and there were two little peafowl chicks as a reward for my broken sleep and early-morning sprints. We wondered if they were a pigeon-pair, that is, a male and a female, and discussed whether to keep them or sell them as a bit of profit. When they were about two days old, we noticed uneasily that Sultan had taken to spending his days crouched just outside the wire netting which surrounded Dingley Dell. Time and again, we chased him away but, next time we looked, it was to find him back at his post. We comforted ourselves with the fact that both parents were protectively attentive to the offspring. The peahen kept them close, clucking and ushering them into the shelter of the bushes, while her mate would raise his tail and rattle it threateningly at the cat. Sultan, however, sensed that he was out of reach, and remained crouched, gazing at the chicks, as though hypnotised.

We had just begun to congratulate ourselves that, after almost a week, they had grown too big to squeeze through the netting, when disaster struck. Their parents lowered their guard simultaneously, and the chicks popped through the holes. It was over in a flash.

57

Before we could do anything to prevent it, Sultan had pounced, and the two chicks lay dead.

We were heartbroken but, as Cyril said, it was his nature to hunt, and we couldn't change it.

It finished our flirtation with exotic species, once and for all. We felt that we couldn't face the spring again, with the noise and hassle, so we made use of our favourite column and advertised them, finding a more remote home, where the peacock could call to his heart's content or perhaps, should I say, to his heart's delight.

CHAPTER SIX

I've said it once, and I'll say it again, Cyril and I are suckers for livestock. Consequently, whenever our nannies, Dinky and Dinah, gave birth, we were always reluctant to part with the kids. We never advertised them but found good homes through fellow goat enthusiasts. There only had to be one which was especially appealing, or unusually marked, and we found every excuse under the sun to keep her.

We realised, of course, that with so little land, there was an absolute limit to the number of kids we could hang on to. We did discuss moving, but in a rather desultory and half-hearted way. The house was, by now, in our eyes at any rate, perfect, and I, in particular, felt that I couldn't bear to leave it, especially after the years of hard work which we'd put into its transformation.

When Cyril picked me up from school, on the day we broke up for Spring Bank Holiday, there was an air of excitement about him and a gleam in his eyes that I hadn't seen for some time. I hadn't even settled in the car, before his enthusiasm bubbled over.

"Storwood Manor's for sale," he announced, "The sign's only gone up today."

I couldn't really see that it should concern us, and almost said so. The hamlet of Storwood was on our route between Cottingwith and York, and consisted of a couple of cottages, about three farms, and the manor house. This was a large, and rather gaunt-looking house, late Georgian, or very early Victorian, standing stark and, to my eyes, ugly on a right-angle bend in the road.

"Surely he couldn't be mad enough to even consider buying it?" I thought. I was wrong!

"I've always liked it," he went on, "and there's more land."

There it was again, the land-hunger of a man bred to farming. My heart sank, but I said nothing. I wasn't even listening as he went on about its merits, sensing my disapproval, and trying to convince me.

As we approached it along the road, I looked at it with fresh eyes, consideringly. No, I couldn't like it. Compared with our pretty, white cottage, it had nothing to recommend it. Anyway, I consoled myself, it would be far too expensive — far beyond our reach.

When he arrived home, Cyril said: "I think I'll ring Mr. Brownridge, and ask if we can view it on Sunday morning."

59

Storwood Manor, a rather gaunt-looking house.

I could think of no logical reason for the panic which rose in me, nor for the hostility I felt towards the house, but I knew that I must register my protest.

"I've never liked the house!" I blurted out. At Cyril's look of amazement, I continued: "I think it's ugly."

"Ugly?" He was incredulous. "It's a magnificent house, and stands well."

With that, he went into the hall, and I could hear him making arrangements to view the property.

We had, by now, been at 'Rose Dene' for several years. Our daughter, Paula, who was a schoolgirl when we had bought it, had married straight from college, and was now living in London. Martin, our son, had a business as a wood carver in a nearby town and was also engaged to be married. This meant that Cyril and I had no one to consider but ourselves. I knew too, that the winding mile-and-a-half from Storwood to our home was the bit of the journey from York which Cyril had always disliked. As well as any other advantage the manor may have, this would be a bonus point to him if, by any remote chance, we could buy it.

Paula, her husband, Clive, and baby, Imogen, arrived on the

Saturday, for the week, and Cyril told them of the arrangement he'd made to view the manor on the next day. Although they both loved the cottage, Paula, who'd known Storwood Manor since her school bus used to stop at the gate, was obviously impressed.

As the property had not yet been advertised, except by means of the agent's board, we were the first viewers. I should think that the Brownridges wondered what had struck them when we trooped in. In addition to ourselves, we took Paula, Clive, and the baby, and also Martin, his fiancée, Lesley, and her little girl by her previous marriage. Looking back, I suppose, it was rather a nerve on our part but, at the time, we needed the support of our family in what seemed to be a big step.

Mr. and Mrs. Brownridge, like us, had a grown-up family and, there only being the two of them at home, they only occupied the back of the house and had for many years rented off the front half. Consequently, it was what had originally been the 'servants' quarters' that we saw first.

I was unimpressed.

Compared with my own charming home, it merely merited a 'Fair' on its report as yet. From the living room, we passed into an inner hall, and then through a second door, into the main hall. A surprise was in store. We grouped round the front door and gazed round in awed silence. The outside of the house gave no indication of the grandeur of the hall and staircase. The sun streamed through the stained glass in the front door and fell upon a beautiful mosaic floor. The wide staircase swept round in almost a full circle, to a galleried landing. It was like something out of a film, and I could imagine one of Georgette Heyer's heroines pausing at the top to make an impact before rustling down to meet the hero waiting at the bottom to escort her into dinner.

Nobody spoke.

When I broke the silence, my remark was so banal as to be an insult to the place.

"How much wallpaper does it take?"

I never did get an answer to the question, as everybody else began to express wonder and admiration. With mounting excitement, we viewed the other front rooms. The drawing-room was almost square, typically Georgian, and beautifully proportioned. Its focal point was a marble fireplace. The mantlepiece was marred with splodges of candle-grease, but nothing could detract from its

61

graceful proportions. I mentally tagged it with the label 'great possibilities,' before proceeding to the next room.

This was the dining-room, which measured twenty-seven feet by eighteen, with four tall, sash windows. While everyone else exclaimed at the impressive size, I mentally worried about the cost of curtains and carpets. By the time we'd traipsed behind Mr. Brownridge in an exploratory column, up the front stairs, through the six bedrooms and bathroom, and down the back stairs, we were still completely lost.

"How on earth do you find your way round?" I asked. He looked surprised. "Oh, it's easy," came the answer.

Despite myself, I liked the house, and could see that everyone else was totally enamoured.

Now for the outside! I suppose from a male point of view, this was really of the most importance.

I often think of my mother-in-law's tale of her first home. One day her future father-in-law had taken the prospective bridegroom to buy a farm. On their return, they'd enthused about the land and the buildings, until she could stand the suspense no longer.

"What's the house like?" she demanded.

Grandad Sunley had eyed her in amazement. "The house?" he echoed, "We never went in, lass. The house isn't important."

Well, the house is important to my husband, I'm pleased to say, but I knew the land and buildings would have equal pull.

Even I was impressed when we went round the buildings, which were set on three sides of a good fold-yard, half of which was roofed over. To our delighted gaze, they seemed to go on for ever — pig sties, calf-houses, loose boxes, a huge barn which, though almost roofless, was surrounded by massive walls. There was even a little cow-house, with standings for six cows and a dairy opening off. To crown it all, there was a mill with a granary above. This was complete with all the antique grinding mechanism.

We daren't, of course, allow our enthusiasm to show. It's not good business tactics. At least, not when you're on the buying side.

There was, however, more to come! With the house there were just four acres. All the other land was to be sold to farmers who had leased it. Perhaps, for our sakes, it would have been better had these four acres been rented off. Mr. Brownridge had not farmed the land for twelve years and to come face to face with Nature, allowed to run unchecked for that length of time, was an awesome sight. We had

The land defied description.

considered 'Rose Dene' to be neglected, but this defied description. Not only were there the usual range of weeds native to the area, but also saplings, shrubs and bushes, self-seeded from the surrounding woodland. Apart from two little fields of less than one acre each, and an orchard, the rest of the land fell away steeply from the house, forming a long valley, and then rose again to a wooded strip along the bank of a canal. To our delighted gaze, there was so much of it, and it was so picturesque, that we ignored the fact that a great deal of it was ings land, or water meadows, and was therefore unusable in winter.

Whereas 'Rose Dene' had been viewed early in the year, before the weeds had begun to flourish, here we saw them in all their glory. Thistles, nettles, rushes and reeds pressed in on us, chest-high. On me, actually, they were head-high, and I trailed back to the house, having lost the others. I could hear their voices, but I was so engulfed in vegetation that sight of them was impossible.

Not for the first time in my life, I began to wonder if we were mad. The prospect of tackling it seemed daunting, to say the least, but we had managed to work wonders on 'Rose Dene,' both as regards the house and the land.

"It's got great possibilities," mused Cyril, on the way home.

I had to admit he was right, but, "D'you think we're too old to do the work?" I ventured.

"Nonsense!" he protested. "We're only in our fifties! We've a great untapped supply of energy inside us."

"Yes, but how do we actually break into it?" I grinned. He grinned back, knowing he'd won the day.

As it was a Bank Holiday weekend, we were forced to contain ourselves in patience until the Tuesday when the estate agent reopened. Unlike the Walkers, when we'd bought 'Rose Dene,' Mr. Brownridge wouldn't talk business, being content to leave it to the agent.

Of course, it was the main topic of conversation over the weekend. I seemed to be the only unenthusiastic one in the whole family.

Of course I could see its potential.

Of course I could see that it had great possibilities.

Of course I'd like to keep more animals — But!!

In the back of my mind, there was always a niggling doubt. First it was one thing, then it was another. It was nine years since we'd tackled 'Rose Dene,' and I wasn't sure about this project. Not only was the house huge, but we knew the extent of the neglect of the land. Cyril was sure that it was within our capabilities to restore house, land and buildings. I, who was usually the optimist, was less sure.

"Come on, love," teased Cyril, "Wouldn't you like to be the Lady of the Manor?"

There was a thought. Would we really be the Lord and Lady of the Manor and, if so, were the titles accompanied by any responsibilities or even, perhaps, privileges?

Monday was hot and sunny so, in the afternoon, we took a gentle stroll along the towpath, to examine Storwood Manor from a different viewpoint. We'd never walked so far along the canalbank before, and discovered a whole new world of peace and tranquillity. The path ran between the canal and a narrow, but deep, beck. Beyond the beck was an extensive bird sanctuary, and our walk was punctuated by bird-spotting and exclaiming over species of wild flowers I hadn't seen since childhood.

Suddenly, above the trees on the opposite bank, we caught our first glimpse of the house. Seen from this angle, it was certainly imposing. The front was typically Georgian, standing high and

64

square, with a south-facing aspect. It was undoubtedly more impressive than the side view from the road.

The trees on the canalbank were mainly willow, huge and aged; some of them leaning out over the water. They were so close together and the undergrowth so thick, that there was very little of the house and buildings open to view. What I had seen, however, had aroused my interest more than the extensive viewing of the previous day.

On the walk home, we discussed it again, I with more interest and warmth; Cyril, oddly enough, less enthusiastic than he had been. There was nothing to be done until next day and, at least, I thought, it had enlivened the weekend. We'd all satisfied the nosiness one had about other people's homes, and Cyril had flirted with the idea of being a Lord of the Manor.

That's all it would amount to, I consoled myself, glancing smugly around my own cosy home, as I went up to bed.

Next morning, with the extra help, Cyril raced through his chores. Milking, feeding, cleaning out and staking out the goats seemed to be done in a flash and, before I could gather my wits, he was on the 'phone to the estate agent.

"Now we're faced with a problem," he remarked on his return to the kitchen. I paused over my pouring of the coffee.

"Why? What do you mean?"

"They're asking very little more for Storwood than we could get for this. It's within our reach. What do you say?" he replied.

I didn't really know what to say. My safe, comfortable little world was being attacked. We'd bought 'Rose Dene' with retirement in mind, and I hadn't anticipated living anywhere else, for the rest of my life. On the other hand, Storwood Manor was a very prestigious house, and the land and buildings were the answer to our dreams.

I've always been a decisive person, quick to make up my mind, and no regrets. Now, however, I was dithering, unable to decide. Was this indecisiveness a sign of senility? I wondered. I was, after all, a grandmother in my fifties. Could I possibly do the work that was required? Cyril seemed to have no fears on that score, so perhaps my fears were groundless.

In the end, we decided that it was too good a chance to miss. Our own property was the type that was selling well, so we thought we'd have a go at something which offered more scope. Not wanting to be caught in a private auction, Cyril put a time-limit of forty-eight hours on his offer, so we weren't kept hanging on long for a decision. Once committed, we'd have felt disappointed, nay, even deprived, if we'd missed the property. However, once more, Fate was on our side (or was it? I was never really sure!). Whichever way our luck fell, our offer was accepted and we were the future owners of Storwood Manor.

Cyril looked appraisingly as his trusty old rotovator, and decided that it just wasn't capable of tackling four acres. The alternative had to be a tractor of some kind. We weren't, however, in the big league, so began to comb the lists of items on offer at small farm sales. One day, fortune smiled on us. At least, she can certainly have the benefit of the doubt, on this occasion. We set off on a beautifully sunny day to a sale about fifteen miles away.

Laid out in a field were rows and rows of farm implements, including several tractors. Right at the end of the row, looking rather shabby and forlorn, was our target, namely a little grey Fergy. I say 'grey' because that's how they're always known but, in a misguided effort to make it appear more modern, someone had daubed it with red paint. Some of the original grey showed here and there and she was undoubtedly battered. To our consternation, while all the other tractors had their engines running, and were either roaring loudly or ticking over, she stood mute.

"Doesn't she work?" I asked.

Cyril consulted his catalgoue. "According to this, she's a 'go-er'," he answered, hurrying away to find somebody in charge. Martin had gone off poking round the fascinating oddments always to be found at country sales, so I stood beside the Ferguson tractor, keeping her company. All the larger, newer, glossier tractors had their complement of small boys scrambling over them and potential buyers, or otherwise, stooping examining their innards. 'Ours,' however, stood alone and ignored. If she worked, I hoped this was a sign in our favour. Surely nobody else could want her, except as a museum-piece, I thought.

Cyril returned, accompanied by a man with a clip-board.

Obviously, here was someone of importance, by his manner. He climbed up on to the tractor, placed his heel against a button on the side of the gearbox, moved the gear-lever to the right then forward. The engine coughed, turned over, and then subsided once more, into silence. The man looked nonplussed.

Suddenly, one of the small boys, playing on a nearby tractor, looked across, spotted our predicament, and ran over to us. Casually, he pressed a button on what I later found out to be the injector pump.

"Try it now, mister," he grinned, looking up with a cheeky smile.

Rather red in the face, the man tried it again and, to the amazement of us all, she roared into life. No sooner had she started, than a large number of onlookers drifted over and stood round. I did so hope that her liveliness hadn't aroused their acquisitive instincts as, in my mind, she was already labelled as 'ours.'

In the distant corner of the field, the auctioneer had already begun his patter, as he moved from lot to lot.

"There's a four-wheeled trailer would just fit behind her," Martin volunteered to Cyril, as they moved away. I knew there were some small lots in which Cyril was interested, but I intended to keep a place by the little Ferguson tractor.

Farm sales are quite different from other sales. Obviously, the lots can't be held up, as in a saleroom, so the auctioneer moves from lot to lot, with his attendant clerical staff. The small lots are usually dealt with first, otherwise the buyers would drift away before these were sold. As other farmers in a district often use the sale as an opportunity to get rid of all their rubbish, the small lots consist of a weird and wonderful assortment whose uses are often a mystery. The auctioneer usually knows most of his clientele, and if he's spotted a scrap dealer among the crowd, many lots of miscellaneous junk are often knocked down without a bid. 'Mr. Smith, 50p,' being the cry, repeated several times.

Once indeed, at a sale nearer home, the auctioneer had turned first to Cyril and then to Martin, who were at opposite sides of the crowd.

"Come on, then!" he protested, "which of you is it to be?"

Turning to Martin, he went on, "You're bidding against your Dad, you know!" Since then, we've tried to stay together at country sales.

On this day, however, I was quite pleased to sit on the grass, enjoying the sunshine and watching the auction draw steadily nearer. At last, they reached the tractors. I was rather shattered at the prices fetched by the first couple of gleaming monsters. I knew that second-hand tractors were expensive, but thousands of pounds were bandied about as if it were Christie's or Sotheby's. I stood up as the throng approached 'our' tractor. Cyril and Martin joined me.

"A genuine little Ferguson tractor – a collector's piece."

"We've got the rully," whispered Cyril.

A rully is the East Yorkshire name for a trailer. I could see complications here. What could we do with a large farm trailer if we didn't manage to buy the tractor? In my mind, the words went round to the tune of 'Drunken Sailor':

"What shall we do with a four-wheeled trailer?"

Cyril glanced at me as I giggled. "What's up, love?"

"Nothing," I murmured, and had no time to say more.

"A genuine little Ferguson tractor. A collector's piece. Always reliable. Who'll start me at three hundred?"

The auctioneer had started his spiel right next to me.

"Three hundred?" I felt sick, and glanced towards Cyril. He just smiled reassuringly, and, indeed, the auctioneer's demands were already diminishing, in leaps and bounds.

"Go on, then! Two hundred and fifty! Two hundred! One! Who'll give me a hundred quid."

Cyril glanced round and he offered: "Fifty."

The auctioneer looked unbelieving. "Fifty!" in feigned amazement.

He paused dramatically. "Oh, all right!" he continued. At that signal, those interested parties who had up to now held back, were galvanised into action. Almost as swiftly as he'd come down, the auctioneer began to go up. "Fifty! Seventy-five! One hundred!" I gulped. I knew that we'd decided that two hundred was as far as we could go. I decided that I'd try to signal to Cyril to go to two-fifty, but, before I could catch his eye, the bidding stopped.

"All done at one hundred and fifty!" called the auctioneer. "Name?" as he walked on to the next lot.

"Sunley," came Cyril's voice.

I realised that I'd been holding my breath. Now it came out as a sigh of relief. We grinned at each other and, while Cyril went to pay for his purchase, Martin took me to see what else they'd bought. It was then I discovered how determined Cyril had been to obtain his little Fergy.

In addition to a few troughs, hand tools and the trailer, he'd also bought two five-gallon cans of diesel to get the tractor home.

While Cyril was in the office, Martin and I loaded the rest of the purchases on to the trailer, ready for him to bring the tractor round. When the tractor and trailer were coupled, Cyril manoeuvred them out of the field and on to the road, accompanied by an ironic cheer from the buyers of more opulent vehicles.

While Martin set off on the tractor, we went back to the car.

"We'll give him time to get a bit ahead," said Cyril, "then, when we've passed him, we'll stop every few miles for him to catch up."

We'd decided on this plan, in case we'd bought a dud, and the tractor broke down on the way. Catching up took longer than expected, as he was by no means crawling. As we overtook, it was to a thumbs up sign from Martin, and waves and cheers from the car.

After a couple of stops for him to come into view, Cyril remarked, "We'll stop in this lay-by until he arrives, and then we'll do a swap — I'd like to know how she handles."

Do men ever grow up? He'd already seen how she handled in the sale field and through the farmyard. However, I suppose he felt it was his 'turn.'

Martin was loath to get down from his perch, but I expect he realised the justice of Dad having a go.

We followed the same procedure as before, until we were only a few miles from home. Then, when the car stopped, Cyril signalled for us to wait. "Here you are, Martin. You can take her the rest of the way."

69

Martin needed no second telling. He was out of the car and on to the tractor in a jiffy. For my part, I couldn't understand my husband's point. Was it that he didn't want to be seen driving her through the village? Surely not. Everyone has a soft spot for the little Fergy. Surely, he'd be proud to own one. However, this wasn't the reason for his crafty swap. From his seat high on the tractor, he'd spotted what we, in the car, couldn't see. Black clouds were gathering on the horizon and before we reached home, the heavens opened and Martin, on the open tractor, was drenched to the skin.

He bore no grudge, however, probably presuming that his drenching was due to an act of fate, rather than the machinations of his wily Dad, and offered to drive the tractor and trailer up to an implement shed at the manor, where Cyril had arranged to keep it. When they both returned, Cyril described with envious enthusiasm the amount of grass and brushwood going to waste at Storwood, while the goats had almost peeled our land bare.

The Brownridges had become involved in a property chain, where everyone is held up by just one buyer. Consequently, the summer, a very hot and dry one, was dragging on, and our removal date seemed to be no nearer.

Having got a foot in the door, Cyril took another step. He approached Mr. Brownridge with a plea based on our shortage of grass. Could we tether our goats on the land at Storwood? "Of course!" came the reply. "You're only too welcome!"

Indeed, not only were our goats welcome but, rather than find some way of transporting them, daily, we were offered accommodation to bed them down in the buildings.

"That's a relief," sighed Cyril, and promptly began to plan the goats' move for the coming Saturday. Luckily, the weather remained fine, and we set off to walk our little herd the mile-and-a-half from Cottingwith to Storwood. Cyril, as befits the patriarch, strode out at the front with Billy. The other goats were led by all the volunteers we could muster, and I brought up the rear, with a skittish goatling called Sadie.

"Now take it slowly," advised Cyril, "There's no hurry, and our only worry is the traffic."

This was certainly true as, though the lane was narrow and exceedingly winding, local traffic didn't give it the respect it deserved, and tended to swoop round the curves at top speed.

It was all right for Cyril to tell us to take it slowly. He merely had to stroll beside the stately Billy whereas I, at the tail-end of the caravan, was struggling with a defiant Sadie.

This was her first venture out of the garden, and it seemed to have gone to her head. First, it was the sound of her hooves on the road which intrigued her. She looked around, as though wondering if that noise could really be coming from her feet. She pattered and leapt, making, it seemed, as much noise as possible. Next, she spotted the luscious hedgerows at the roadside. When she first tugged towards the hedge, I allowed her to stop and browse. That this was a mistake on my part was obvious almost immediately.

As the others vanished round a bend, I twitched Sadie's lead as a signal for her to move after them. She didn't even turn to give me a look, but rolled her eyes, looking at me out of the corners, and reached up for even more succulent tips of hawthorn.

Although they look graceful and delicate, even young goats are immensely strong, and it took all my strength to part Sadie from her snack.

Having fallen behind the main convoy, of course, I put on a spurt to catch up. Sadie, however, continued to strain, first towards one side of the road, and then the other, intent on reaching the tempting branches. It took all the force I could muster to yank her back into the road, and our progress was rather like a yacht tacking along a river. Rarely did we go forward, but wavered from side to side, like a drunken boat-horse, as the saying goes. Occasionally, I saw the others ahead, strolling nonchalantly at a sedate pace, while Sadie and I struggled along, getting further and further behind. My shoulder joints felt red-hot and sweat was pouring from my brow in a most unladylike manner. So perverse was the goat that, if I heard a car, and tried to coax, or even drag her on to the grass verge, she dug in her heels and remained obstinately in the middle of the road. How we escaped with our lives, I didn't really know.

Eventually, the chimneys of the manor came into view above the trees. I've never been more thankful to spot anything in my life. Before we reached our destination, we had to pass White Cross Farm. Sadie's exertions had just begun to take their toll on her and she'd slowed to a walk about a hundred yards back. Seeing the buildings, she evidently decided that this was where she'd been heading. Slowly, she sank to the ground outside the farmhouse, and refused to move. Although it was her own fault, I did feel a certain sympathy towards her. If I'd given way to my feelings, I'd have lain

71

down beside her and gone to sleep. As it was, I knew she was too heavy to carry, and I must get her to her feet, and walking again. I begged, pleaded, coaxed and cajoled.

Sadie raised one eyebrow and yawned.

That did it!

"Come on you!" I shouted.

With a great yank, I pulled on her lead. Reluctantly, she staggered to her feet and together we tottered the last couple of hundred yards.

When we'd bedded down the goats and given them a generous helping of hay, they snuggled down in comfort while we, poor fools, retraced our steps and walked all the way back again. Nobody but me seemed to be suffering any ill-effects, so I plodded on in silence, putting one burning foot in front of the other, with teeth grimly clenched. I wasn't going to be the only one to complain of aching feet and exhaustion, but, I'm afraid, for the rest of our acquaintance, Sadie remained one of my least favourite goats we ever possessed.

Week followed week, and our completion date seemed as far away as ever. This was awkward to say the least, as we'd arranged to have Martin and Lesley's wedding reception in the dining-room of our new home. The invitations had been sent out, and the time was drawing perilously close to the chosen day. Eventually, the Brownridges offered to move out, if they could pack most of their furniture in the drawing-room. We felt rather guilty but exceedingly grateful for their gesture. We at last arranged to move at the weekend before the wedding. Cyril rather shattered me, by saying that he considered a removal firm a waste of money.

"After all, we've got the tractor and trailer," he remonstrated.

I was a trifle disturbed at the thought of my bits and pieces exposed to the gaze of the whole village.

"Oh, what the heck!" I exclaimed realising that the hundred pounds, or so, could be better spent.

Luckily, we were again blessed with the weather, and every trip to attend to the goats was accompanied by a car-load of things not in regular use. When the Saturday arrived, Cyril and Martin made journey after journey with trailer-loads of furniture. The last load, at tea-time, bore me, Martin, Lesley, and little two-year-old Tammy seated on the settee atop a trailer-load, waving in regal fashion to everyone we passed. Thus we left East Cottingwith after nine years, confirming what the villagers had always believed, that the Sunleys were totally crackers.

CHAPTER SEVEN

Our first winter at Storwood Manor was, typically, the coldest for years. Although we considered ourselves to be hardy, we had grown used to the comfort of central heating, which cushions one from the outside elements. Now, memories of our childhood were evoked, when going upstairs into the bedrooms was a thing to delay as long as possible. I remember that my mother's false teeth often froze in their glass of water on the bedside table.

Like the Brownridges before us we were reduced to spending most of our time in the breakfast room, as we found it impossible to heat the dining-room. However, there was plenty to keep us busy, both inside and out. Cyril plodded on, repairing buildings, and we tackled the decorating of the inside of the house.

"I don't know how we're going to get the place warm for Christmas," worried Cyril. We'd already decided that, now we had plenty of room, we were going to have a real old-fashioned family Christmas.

"We can always have fires in the bedrooms," I suggested.

From the look on Cyril's face, I think he considered this to be the ultimate in decadence. To me, a fire in the bedroom is one of life's luxuries. In childhood, I'd lived in a mining village where coal was plentiful and cheap, and fires in bedrooms were an accepted part of life. It's such a comforting, cosy feeling to lie in bed, watching the firelight flickering on the ceiling, and gradually drifting off to sleep.

We eventually decided that, as long as the menfolk carried the fuel up and the ashes down, fires in the bedrooms it would be.

We invested in a mobile gas heater, to boost the warmth given out by the dining-room fire, and decided that life would be bearable for our Christmas guests.

I think the worst thing that first winter was taking a bath. The bathroom was larger than any room we'd had in 'Rose Dene,' and its only window, a large sash one, was not only ill-fitting, but faced due east. Consequently, this was the coldest room in the house.

The bath was a huge, old-fashioned one and, as the system was served by the breakfast room fire, which never went out, there was always a constant supply of piping-hot water. Getting into the bath was, therefore, no problem. The technique was to fill the bath as full as possible, with water as hot as we could bear. It only took a couple

73

of minutes to scramble out of one's clothes and into the warm water. The crunch came, of course, when it was time to get out.

I used to wallow in the warmth, debating whether the room would be as chilly as the time before. Even the steam didn't seem to do much to raise the temperature in the room, and plucking up one's courage to climb out was always an effort.

I've heard it said that the Finns run out and roll in the snow after a sauna, which practice leaves them glowing with health. I'm afraid a frantic towelling in an icy bathroom, followed by a quick sprint down a long, chilly corridor, did nothing for me. True, I did appreciate the warmth of an electric blanket when I actually reached my bed, but bathing in those conditions was not a régime I'd recommend. It did, however, stiffen our resolve that come what may, before the next winter, we'd afford some form of central heating, and a second, smaller bathroom.

Before moving to Storwood, as I've said, we had wondered whether being 'Lord of the Manor' carried any status. We never really did get an answer to the question, but had a sneaking feeling that our new home may have been responsible for a visitation which we had, one evening.

It was a crisp, frosty night, and we'd pulled the settee across the front of the fire, when there was a knock at the door. Cyril answered it to find two men standing there.

"Evening, Maister, can we 'ave a word?"

"Of course, come in," replied my husband, moving aside to allow the couple of men to enter. As I'd never set eyes on either one before, I couldn't help but feel that this was rather a foolish move on his part.

"Evening, Missus. I 'opes as 'ow your 'ens is fastened up. Old Reynard's on the loose. We passed 'im on the road," said the older man, with a movement I can only describe as touching his forelock.

This was so out of context with the modern world, that I felt like a character in a pantomime — enter two villagers, Left.

"Would you be so kind as to sign Tommy's gun licence application, sir?" came the request.

"Of course," answered Cyril, stretching out his hand for the document.

Another foolhardy move! They could be bank robbers for all we knew, I thought, never stopping to consider that criminals certainly wouldn't bother with gun licences.

74

When Cyril had signed it, he read it through and then frowned. "Just a minute," he said, and went into the kitchen. Looking after him I saw him, out of the men's view, motioning me to follow him.

"His suspicions are aroused," I thought, but turned and smiled at the two men.

"Excuse me," I said, and hurried after him, feeling that he should have gone through to the hall, where the 'phone was.

"What's wrong?" I whispered.

"What are my qualifications?" he hissed, "I can't put 'Lord of the Manor'."

For a moment, I was blank.

"Put 'Parish Concillor'," I whispered, and shot back to keep an eye on the men.

"There you are," he smiled, coming in and handing over the paper.

"Thank you, sir. Goodnight. Goodnight, Missus," and off they went.

"How do you know they should have a gun?" I demanded. "You don't even know them."

"I met them when I was canvassing for the Council. They farm a couple of miles at the other side of Cottingwith," said Cyril, looking astonished at my outburst.

We never knew why they'd ignored other councillors who lived in the village and were, therefore, much nearer. We could only conclude that there was some mystique attached to being 'Lord of the Manor.' Certainly, when we gave our address in shops, we were met with an obsequiousness which we'd never encountered before and could only put down to the impression the Manor had on people.

Christmas came and went, and though we were once or twice cut off from Cottingwith by deep snow, the straight half-mile between us and the main, albeit 'B' class, road, remained open. This meant that we had our old-fashioned family Christmas and, though the weather was cold, we managed to keep the whole house heated, and everyone thoroughly enjoyed the holiday.

Our guests had only just left, however, when it really began to snow in earnest. Remembering our childhood, when snow-ploughs weren't as efficient as nowadays, we stocked up with flour, lard and other staple foods.

Owing to Brownridge's kindness, Cyril had worked at Storwood most of the summer. He'd cleaned about a quarter of an acre of the

Stackyard field, and grown enough vegetables to last over the winter. We had, by now, three large freezers. One contained vegetables and fruit, one held meat, and the other was in one of the buildings neatly stacked with packets of goats' milk. We felt that, even if we were cut off from shops, we could manage to survive.

It was not long after Christmas that we had another pair of visitors. When Cyril answered the door, a very bedraggled young couple were huddled on the doorstep, in a driving snowstorm.

"My car's off the road, and stuck in a snowdrift," explained the young man. I went to put the kettle on, while Cyril brought them in beside the fire. When they were thawed out, hands wrapped round mugs of hot coffee, Cyril got more details. No wonder they were soaked. The car had skidded over a mile away, at a notorious right-angled bend.

Cyril wrapped up warmly, and went to get the tractor and a length of tow-rope. The girl stayed with me while her boy-friend accompanied Cyril on the tractor. Although Cyril loved his little Fergy, he would cheerfully have swapped her for one with a cab that night. As it was, the mile-long journey took what seemed, both to Cyril, who was struggling to see through the blinding snow, and to us by the fire, an eternity.

Luckily, the car was undamaged, merely resting in a snow-filled ditch. The road was filling up rapidly, as Cyril and the lad struggled in almost waist-deep snow to couple up the car to the tractor. Eventually, they managed to get the car out of the ditch, and made their slow way home.

Hearing that they were bound for a party in York, we persuaded them to ring up and cry off. Cyril then gave them directions for another way home, avoiding Storwood Lane, which had been blocking up behind them, as they wound their way back to the house. Once Cyril and the young man were thoroughly warmed through, we waved them off and then crawled wearily up to bed.

When we awoke next morning, there was no improvement in the weather. We'd realised the previous evening that we were cut off from the village. Now it was obvious that there was no way I could get into York to school. Just outside our gate, where the road should be, were undulating drifts of snow, almost chest-deep on me. I'd just telephoned School to explain my predicament, promising to be in as soon as the snow-plough had cleared the road, when there was a knock at the back door.

It was one of the brothers from the neighbouring farm.

"Could Cyril give us a hand?" he gasped.

"Come in a minute," I urged, unable to believe the severity of the weather outside. He hurriedly shook himself, and kicked the snow off his boots, before stepping into the house.

"What's wrong?" asked Cyril, as he came in from the buildings.

"We've got all the sheep under cover, except these in the corner field, and we want to build a shelter of bales," he explained. "Even if we'd room for them, there's no way we could move them in this lot."

"I'll be with you in a minute," said Cyril, as he began to prepare himself for the ordeal. Coat, scarf, woolly hat, seaboot stockings, wellies and gloves were hurriedly put on, and then, taking a deep breath, he launched himself into the storm.

He told me later, that he'd never experienced such appalling conditions. The wind was so strong, that it was almost impossible to draw breath. He pulled his scarf over his nose and mouth, to get some relief, but it made little difference. The wind was howling like a mob of banshees, and I watched anxiously from the breakfast-room window, as he struggled round the corner of the house, towards the tractor and trailer. As the wind caught him, he was brought almost to a standstill, but he managed to make his way through the drifts, following the path made by Keith, our neighbour, though this was rapidly filling up.

The force of the gale was so strong that the snow was being driven almost horizontally, parallel to the ground. I was glued to the window, until they reached the field gate, and turned in. Before they could open it, they had to shovel the snow away and then, making slow progress, the tractor and trailer turned and trundled down into the field.

What they couldn't know, of course, was the depth of the snow on the uneven ground, and they were only just through the gate when the trailer sank up to its axle and couldn't be moved. This meant that the bales had to be placed in the corner of the field, instead of where they had hoped.

I could just catch glimpses of the three figures, through the mist of snow, as they heaved the bales into position.

It was impossible to discern which was which and they were frequently obscured from my view altogether, by the implacable snow, which seemed determined to obliterate them.

They worked in the lee of the trailer to keep out of the biting wind

77

and, as they stumbled through the snow with the bales, they tried to hold them in front of their faces, to obtain some relief from the force of the blizzard.

Although they were only twenty yards from our window, there were times, as I said, when they were lost to my view altogether, so poor was the visibility. The sheep, however, must have sensed their presence, because they began to make their way across the field and gathered round the men as they worked.

The battle took all morning but, eventually, the shelter was finished, and, even as the men mounted the tractor, the grateful sheep huddled behind the bales, close together for warmth.

The trailer was immovable and remained marooned in the field for weeks, but the tractor managed the journey home, dropping Cyril off at our gate. When he came in, he looked as if he'd been South with Scott. Even his eyebrows were snow-encrusted, and his teeth were chattering so much that he couldn't speak.

I helped him off with his outdoor clothes and he crouched by the fire, with a bowl of hot soup.

"We must be out of our minds!" he exclaimed, when he'd recovered enough to talk. "We could be in the comfort of a

The transformation was utterly incredible.

78

centrally-heated house and we're here, having chosen this life, of our own free will."

Later in the afternoon, the storm abated and the sky cleared. The transformation was utterly incredible. Although we knew that the hamlet was isolated and, indeed, we were now cut off from our neighbours at each side, the outlook was breathtakingly beautiful. The drifts of snow were unsullied by traffic and the hedgerows and trees were Christmas-card-like in their iced beauty. When the sun came out, we tried to see how far from the house we could walk, but it was only a few yards before, away from the sheltering house, the drifts were impassable.

We and our animals were encapsuled in a world of tranquillity and beauty. In our little kingdom, we all depended on each other, and we felt as though the world and its troubles had no power to touch us. The feeling of peace which engulfed us made the wild struggle of the morning seem unreal.

"There's one good thing," remarked Cyril. "All our stock's accessible."

Indeed we realised the forethought that had gone into the layout of the house and buildings, grouped around the fold-yard. Although we were surrounded on all sides by drifts, all our own buildings were sheltered, with doors facing inwards, to the yard. This meant that the normal routine of feeding, milking and mucking out could proceed as usual, and our goats remained comfortable and well-tended.

For three days we remainded cocooned in our snow-muffled world. Although the blizzard was over and the days were sparklingly clear, the temperature was so low that the snow showed no sign of melting. We decided, in reluctant disbelief, that the snow-plough team had lost the map which showed the position of Storwood. Actually, on talking it over, we realised that with a population of nine, our little hamlet could wait, while other and larger groups were freed.

On the fourth morning, the silence was broken by the sound of scraping and clanging. Cyril listened a moment to locate the direction.

"It's Tim!" he said and, seizing his shovel, went out of the yard gates to work his way towards him, from our end.

Tim was our neighbour at the other side, whose place was actually away from the road, being reached by a cart-track, which passed through our land. With Cyril working towards him, they soon cleared a path from one house to the other.

"What do you say to trying to reach the main road?" suggested Tim.

"Why?" asked Cyril, who felt very contented with life as it was. "It's over half-a-mile, and most of it blocked solid, the way that wind was blowing," he continued, half-heartedly.

"Well, the snow-plough isn't going to come, and we must do something," Tim protested.

I must admit that I felt quite guilty, being holed up at home, when school was in session, and both Tim and his daughter also needed to get to York, so a plan of action was formed. With a combination of shovels and the tractor, they hoped to gradually clear a way through the lane to the main road. There was no guarantee, of course, that this would be open but, at least, they'd be doing something to relieve the situation.

They looked a comical couple as they started out on their task, rotund from layers of clothing, each topped by a bobble-hat and Tim sporting a pair of Yeti-boots, shaggy and ungainly-looking but undoubtedly warm. Indeed, they looked more suited to the 'Aprés-ski' scene than snow-shifting in Yorkshire.

I doubt very much whether the two men would have tackled the job had they realised what a Herculean labour it was to be. However, once started, there was no turning back. I think that each was afraid to lose face by chickening out, so on they went.

They made slow progress up the lane, by dint of charging each snow-drift with the tractor, until it would go no further, and then digging and loosening the snow with the shovels until the tractor was freed and could make a little more progress.

At last, at about three o'clock, I picked up the 'phone and dialled the school number.

"We've reached the main road, and unless there's more snow tonight, we're going to try to get through to York in the morning," I told the school secretary.

"Oh, Mrs. Sunley, the school's closed! The boiler's broken down. The girls have all been sent home, and I'm just leaving," she answered.

"Oh, well," I thought, as I went back to the fire. "At least I needn't feel guilty any longer."

Apart from the narrow track which Cyril and Tim had dug, the roads remained virtually impassable for days. We could make our way into York, though our slithers and skids were hair-raising, but there was no means of going in the other direction, even to the village, a mile-and-a-half away.

The thaw eventually came, of course, as thaws always do. One day, our surroundings were a fairy-tale picture, bejewelled with diamonds and crystals and the next we were squelching around, ankle-deep in treacherous slush, discovering leaky roofs in buildings which we had congratulated ourselves were sound.

Our ings-land behind the house became soggier and soggier, until I could no longer reach the wooded canalbank, to indulge in one of my favourite occupations: gathering sticks for kindling.

Between trudging round the buildings to do the incessant round of daily chores, feeding, milking and mucking out, Cyril was up ladders, patching and blocking holes in roofs, while my lot seemed to be standing on the bottom rung, straining to hold the ladder upright and steady.

Then the rains came!

All repair work to the buildings was brought to a standstill. Only the bare essentials of outside work were attended to, while any 'spare' time was spent in decorating the inside of the house.

We noticed, of course, that behind the house we now had quite a sizeable lake — indeed, we'd have been blind to miss it. However, when I voiced my disquiet about the size of it, Cyril was comforting in pointing out how much more rain must fall to raise the water level even an inch, over such a large area. After two or three days of heavy rain, I felt that I could relax when, at last, the skies cleared and the rain stopped.

The very next evening, we were disturbed by a smart rap on the door. Upon opening it, I found myself facing two policemen, clad in raincoats and carrying torches.

"Are you all right, love?" asked one.

Wondering why we shouldn't be, I assured them that we were.

"Have you looked out at the back, tonight?" persisted his companion.

"N-no," I answered, "not since tea-time," wondering what could be wrong.

"What's the matter, constable?" enquired Cyril, who had joined me at the door.

"May we come in a minute, sir?"

81

"Of course."

Once in, they went through the breakfast-room and into the kitchen.

"Is this the back door?" enquired the first officer, as he drew the bolts.

When he threw open the door, we crowded into the opening, peering out in disbelief and amazement.

As they swept the ings with their torches, we could see nothing but water, reaching to within about ten teet of the house.

"The river and canal have burst their banks. They couldn't take the amount of flood-water that's swept down," explained one of the men. "Do you think you'll be safe tonight?"

"Oh, yes, don't worry about us," Cyril assured him. "This house has stood here for over a hundred and fifty years, and never been flooded yet."

"There's always a first time," I added silently, as we saw them out.

Despite my doubts, Cyril was adamant in his faith in the house.

While I contemplated the making of one or two sandbags, just for the back door and dairy window, Cyril reiterated the statement he'd made when we'd first discussed buying the manor.

"It stands well," he declared. "We'll be fine, you'll see."

I must admit that he was right. The house did stand well and we were fine. When next morning we looked out of the upstairs windows at the back of the house though, we were in for a shock. Where we had been used to a vista of green, now stretched what we later found out to be six miles of water.

When we had first moved into the area, I had considered the flat countryside to be dull and monotonous. As the rolling acres of West Yorkshire had been my childhood home, I had consequently grown to regard hilly countryside as a prerequisite to beauty. It took the chance remark of a Scottish visitor to make me regard my surroundings in a fresh light.

"How glorious to have extensive views, instead of being hemmed in on all sides by hills!" was the exclamation which had taken me by surprise.

Now, oddly enough, when the view to the west was a vista consisting almost entirely of water, I found the contemplation of it both soothing and absorbing. The upper skeletons of the trees rose from the water, their mirrored images shimmering and wavering in the lightest breeze. The clouds scudded across the blue water as

Six miles of water.

fitfully and lightly as in the sky above. The ings beyond the canal were a nature reserve, the stopping off place for thousands of migratory birds, so that we had constantly-changing compositions of trees, water and birds to delight our days.

Best of all were the sunsets. We had always had magnificent sunsets at Storwood, a whole palette of colours. Some nights we were delighted by glorious blazes of oranges and reds, streaked by light, tawny clouds or, alternatively, heavy coppery masses. On other evenings, we enjoyed no less impressive but more subtle sunsets, ranging from deep indigo to the palest and most delicate violet or even turquoise and eau-de-nil. Now these delights were doubled; the black tree-shapes rising from the water which reflected every hue, tint and shade one could imagine. We never tired of gazing and drinking in the beauty.

As long as we remained at the manor, I would never again long for the hills. I looked out to the horizon and revelled in the distance laid out to my view.

CHAPTER EIGHT

During the long, cold winter months, it was brought home to us, in no uncertain manner, that there was no way we were going to be able to live in Storwood Manor, during another winter, without the benefit of some form of background heating. We wanted to enjoy the whole of the lovely old house, and not spend our winters hibernating in the servants' quarters, cosy though they were.

We weighed up the various methods of heating the whole house, knowing full well that, taking into account the fact that our outgoings usually, more or less, balanced our income, it must of necessity be a do-it-yourself job.

We avidly pored over self-sufficiency books and magazines, contemplating solar energy (not enough sun!), wind-power (too many trees, shielding the windmill!) and every other scheme, be they possible, improbable, or just plain hare-brained.

For almost a fortnight, during which my hair turned visibly greyer, Cyril mulled over the possibility of using the septic tank to produce methane gas. He covered sheets of paper with diagrams, sketches and notes to work out how many pigs, sheep and calves we'd need in addition to our existing stock, to produce enough gas to heat the house.

Although my husband and I usually see eye-to-eye, I must admit that I could raise no enthusiasm for this plan. Indeed, to say I was uneasy was an understatement. Apprehension was too mild a word to sum up my feelings towards this project — terror was more the term! No matter how many articles I read about people who had successfully harnessed this energy, in my opinion, the only outcome of this experiment would be an inevitable explosion. I wasn't sure in my mind as to the size of the explosion. It varied from day to day, from a megaton event, which would demolish the whole property (including us) to a rather lesser bang which would shower us, and the surrounding countryside, with the unspeakably horrible contents of the septic tank.

In the end, common sense prevailed. The fuel of which we had an abundance was wood. A wood-burning stove, then, would form the basis of the scheme to heat our home. I must admit that our final decision was influenced by the fact that we were given the chance to buy a wood-burner cheaply.

When we arrived to collect our purchase, it was standing in the open air, behind the house, looking very sad, dilapidated and rusty. When the owner saw Martin's van, he was openly derisive.

"It would have been sold long ago, and for a lot more money, but nobody could move it," he explained.

"You'll never get it in that van," he continued, smugly.

The three of us looked at each other and grinned. Cyril and Martin unloaded two huge planks of elm, which they propped up on the back of the van to act as a ramp. I, meanwhile, had armed myself with some pieces of scaffold to use as rollers.

The man looked on, goggle-eyed, as with expertise born of practice, the menfolk tipped the stove on to one of the rollers and proceeded to roll it along the drive up the planks and into the van. My job was to pick up each roller from the rear of the operation, as the stove moved on and away, and then run and place it in front.

No doubt the whole proceedings looked like something performed in a circus, by a trio of clowns, but it works! Cyril always insists that the stones of Stonehenge were moved by rollers and, certainly, we, as a family, were never backwards in coming forwards where the use of rollers is concerned. We've moved aviaries, sheds and machinery, and now we trundled the stove into the van with ease, leaving its previous owner speechless in amazement.

The installation of the stove and its attendant heating system occupied Cyril during the rest of the winter months. He also converted the smallest bedroom into a most luxurious bathroom, complete with shower. Now not only did we feel that we could face future winters with equanimity, but there was the added bonus of taking paying guests for farm holidays, if we ever needed to do so.

Once the grass began to grow, the goats were staked out, but it soon became obvious that there was far too much herbage for even them to keep cropped. We were, however, in for a pleasant surprise.

Lesley and Martin arrived one afternoon, brimming over with eagerness and obviously bursting to share a secret, but determined to keep us guessing.

"Can you spare an hour or so, to come for a little drive?"

No matter how much we quizzed them we could get nothing out of them. Our questions were merely met with smiles and promises of "You'll see!"

Of course we went. Who wouldn't have done? Our curiosity was fully aroused, as we got into the car and followed their van, to a village about four miles away. As we left the vehicles, to walk up the path of a charming old cottage, Lesley pulled me back.

"We're buying Grandad a 'Jacob's' ewe as an early birthday present," she confided. I was thrilled, but was unsure of Cyril's reaction. As I've mentioned before, he had never been a sheep person, considering them to be stupid. At the same time, he'd lumped sheep and goats together, as equally undesirable animals. Now, however, his herd of goats was the delight of his life, so maybe a sheep wouldn't be an unwelcome gift. We are both keen on the survival of rare breeds, so I knew that, if he was going to keep sheep, he'd prefer 'Jacob's' to the more common breeds kept by the surrounding farmers.

When Martin knocked, the door was opened by a beanpole of a man. He stood well over six feet tall, lean to the point of skinniness. His legs, clad in skin-tight jeans, seemed to stretch for half his height, so that he resembled a human hairpin.

His wife, with whom the appointment had been made, had been called away. He knew where she'd left the two ewes, from whom Cyril was to choose, and led us to the back of the cottage. The land had been divided into wire-nettinged enclosures, in one of which stood the two ewes.

We lined the fence and contemplated them. Glancing at Cyril, I realised immediately that he'd lost his heart. They certainly were pretty little things, dainty and more lightly-built than the huge Leicesters which we were used to seeing in the fields round our house. One, Julie, we were told, had a slight advantage over her sister, Jessica, as far as looks were concerned. Her black markings were more evenly distributed and her face was rather prettier. However, they were two little beauties.

Cyril was overwhelmed with gratitude at the family's thoughtfulness.

"Thank you," he beamed, "I'll have Julie."

He turned to the man.

"And I'll buy Jessica myself," he added. "It would be a shame to separate them."

"Fine!" came the answer, as the lanky legs scissored over the fence to join the sheep.

From his approach, it was instantly obvious that the sheep were his wife's province and that he hadn't the slightest idea of how to deal with animals. As they huddled together in a corner, he bore down on them, arms and legs moving wildly, as though jerked on strings like an outsize puppet.

"Shall we give you a hand?" called Cyril, anxiously.

"No! No! I'll soon catch them!" he threw back over his shoulder, as he swooped down on his prey.

As he made his final lunge towards them, they turned in unison and, with no apparent effort, skipped over the fence and into the next enclosure, leaving him clutching foolishly at thin air.

The bewilderment on his face was ludicrous, until, spotting his quarry, he emitted a strangled "Arrgh!" and once more the amazing legs cut through the air, as he scissor-jumped his way over the intervening obstacle, to enter the fray once again.

His appearance could be summed up in a West Riding phrase of my childhood. "He's like nowt else but a yard o' pump watter!" His elbows stuck out, his knees stuck up, and his head jutted forward and each time the twins skipped gracefully over a fence, he launched himself after them, in such an ungainly fashion that his knees almost hit his chin.

His scarlet face was by now dripping with sweat and his eyes were sticking out, like chapel hat pegs, as the saying is. Our sympathy, however, was not for him, as he constantly rejected shouted offers of assistance.

"No! No! I can manage!"

It was, of course, his pride which was now at stake. He wasn't going to be beaten by a couple of sheep, especially in front of strangers.

Grimly, he swooped on them, time and time again, only to be foiled, at the last moment, by their superior agility.

His physical distress was matched by that of the ewes, though theirs was shown in the way they stayed together, trembling with fright.

"Whoa! Whoa!" Cyril suddenly called, unable to bear the spectacle any longer. The man stopped in his stride and looked round. His chest heaved and he was unable to speak, he was panting so heavily. He did manage, however, to raise his eyebrows interrogatively, while sagging against the fence.

"You'll never catch them," said Cyril, "and you're doing them no good at all."

The man slewed round and regarded the sheep, who eyed him anxiously, while obviously again preparing for flight.

87

"I can't understand it!" he gasped, wiping his forehead with the back of his hand. "My wife never has any trouble with them."

While this conversation was going on, Cyril picked up two lengths of tethering ropes, which the ungainly stockman had forgotten to take with him into the arena.

Motioning Martin to approach the frightened animals from the other side, Cyril gently closed in on them, murmuring soothing sounds and repeating their names.

"Come on, Julie, come, Jessica," he intoned as he crept forward. Working in unison, motivated only by hand signals, the two gradually drew closer to their targets until, with a final plunge, each grasped a sheep by its wool in one hand, while encircling its neck with the other, and heaved them over on to their sides. Once this was done, the victims lay supine and docilely allowed their feet to be tied.

Our host couldn't believe his eyes. That this technique should succeed, when all his energy had been wasted, to no avail, seemed to leave him incredulous. With a visible effort, he pulled himself together and accompanied Lesley and me to the house. There, he recovered sufficiently to take our money, while the men loaded the sheep into the back of the van.

When we reached home, we put them into a loose box to recover from their ordeal, while we sat down to discuss this unforeseen addition to our stock. The venture was not yet over, however.

Just after tea, we received a 'phone call from Julie and Jessica's previous owner.

"I'm sorry I missed you," she apologised, "but I understand from my husband that he caught them without any trouble."

Recalling his gangling progress over fences and through grass, I smiled to myself as I agreed with her.

"What I really wanted to know," she went on, "is whether you would take Joanna off my hands. She's the mother of Julie and Jessica, and she's so old, I'd let you have her for five pounds!"

Sentimental as ever, we agreed to buy Joanna, as long as she was delivered to us, which she duly was, next day.

We were later to discover that Jezebel would have been a more appropriate name for this cunning old girl. She knew every trick in the book!

We had been warned that 'Jacob's' sheep were prodigious jumpers, and almost impossible to keep in the confines of a field. We had seen for ourselves Julie and Jessica's prowess in the high jump,

88

on the day we acquired them. Joanna, however, having lost some of her agility with the onset of old age, had compensated by the use of craftiness. Who said sheep were stupid?

Time and time again she was found in the wrong field. At other times, we observed her from the windows, strolling along the road. Yet again she was reported by passing motorists, who had seen her ambling down the lane. No matter how often Cyril patrolled the perimeter of her paddock, the only clues were places where the wire netting bulged, or had been lifted.

Then, one day, he caught her at it. As he watched from a distance, the wily old thing lay down with her back to the netting and, keeping her horns turned away, she pushed, shoved and shuffled backwards, gradually raising the fence, until she could roll through.

Cyril looked at her, a smile crossing his face.

"If that doesn't beat hen-racing by candlelight, I'm a Dutchman!" This odd expression was one of Cyril's father's. Whenever he was astounded, he would show his incredulity by bursting out with "Well, if that doesn't beat hen-racing by candlelight!" For Cyril to use it was proof of his amazement. "You crafty old thing," he murmured, though he couldn't help but admire her ingenuity. "At least, I know now how you manage it."

From then on, any fence confining Joanna was checked and double-checked to see that it was well pegged down. Even so, there were times when she outwitted him and needed to be recaptured after her perambulations along the road.

When they joined our growing family, although Joanna was in-lamb, Julie and Jessica were still what are known as 'gimmers.' That is, female lambs who are not pregnant and have never given birth. We believed, therefore, that our main problem was the purchase of a 'Jacob's' ram.

Ignorance may not be bliss, but it can sometimes be a comfort, albeit a temporary one. Our ignorance left us untutored in the regulations regarding the shearing and dipping of sheep, omission to do which incurred the penalty of heavy fines. Not for the first time did we thank our lucky stars for the kindness of the neighbouring brothers. When the time came, our small flock was rounded up with their hundreds, for dipping and shearing, without pressure, without fuss and, more important, without charge.

These events, however, necessary as they were, belonged to the future. Our present concern was that neither Julie nor Jessica had been put to the tup. Falling back to our stand-by, the livestock column of the local paper, we soon found what we were seeking.

A quick 'phone call elicited the information that the first-comer would have the choice of no less than three young rams. We therefore set off the next Saturday morning, armed with the usual assortment of sacks and ropes, and the back seat well covered.

"We really must try to afford a trailer," I protested. To us, the car smelt as fresh as a dewy morning, whereas smokers' cars were positively nauseating to our noses. What ours smelt like to any stranger entering it, I didn't care to consider, used as it was for carrying livestock, bags of animal feed and anything else we wished to transport.

Anyway, off we went, well prepared and in a merry mood. Although we had been given what had seemed like explicit instructions over the telephone, the particular area, to the north of York, was unknown territory to us, and the journey took far longer than we'd expected. After having asked the way for the umpteenth time, we caught sight of a farm, in the distance, just as the road looked about to peter out.

It was our destination, thank goodness, and we presumed that we hadn't been alone in having difficulty in finding the farm. Although the farmer's wife had had several enquiries, we were the first to arrive, and so had our choice of the three young rams.

Three times she disappeared into a building, each time reappearing leading a 'Jacob's' ram on a halter. They were paraded for our inspection as proudly as though in the show-ring.

The first was rejected out of hand. Alas, poor fellow, he only had three horns, having knocked one off when he was a baby. Although this was no hindrance to his capabilities as a stud animal, it did give him a lopsided look and spoilt his appearance. Ignoring the fact that this defect may mean a reduction in price, we debated the qualities of the other two.

In the end, we made our choice. Though both were magnificent specimens, one had a certain something which raised him above the other, to our eyes. Although standing quietly by his mistress, his head was held more proudly and there was a gleam in his eye which betokened spirit — or was it defiance?

"That's the one," decided Cyril.

"Good," answered the farmer's wife, "One down and two to go."

We produced our sack and pieces of rope. With quick efficiency, she bundled him into the sack, tying it round his neck, as she slipped off his halter.

"There you are, then," she said, as Cyril heaved him away, to place him in the back of the car. Catching his baleful glare, as I rested the cheque book on the gatepost, I wondered whether we'd chosen rightly. However, consoling myself philosophically that what was done was done, I took my place in the car beside my beaming spouse.

"Isn't he a grand specimen?" gloated Cyril.

Not knowing the finer points of 'Jacob's' sheep, I agreed, before reminding myself that neither did Cyril. However, he certainly did look a grand animal.

We were only about half-way home, when he began to object, in no uncertain manner, to his undignified mode of transport. First he began to wriggle, and then to hurl himself about on the car-seat, doing his best to effect an escape from the constricting sack.

"Now, now," I soothed, as I craned round in my seat to rub his nose. No sooner had my hand reached him, however, than he jerked his head away, with a glower of malevolent detestation on his face.

"Do sheep bite?" I quavered, drawing my hand away, so quickly that my elbow caught Cyril under the ear.

"Look out!" he yelled, as the car swerved. "You'll have us in the ditch!"

"Not half as quickly as Jake will, if he gets loose!" I replied grimly.

Cyril hadn't realised the likelihood of this possibility before, so he pulled in at the next lay-by and inspected the ram's bonds.

"He's all right. They're firm enough, Anyway, we shan't be long, now." So we went on our way.

We'd already decided that any more additions to our little flock would have names beginning with 'J,' as had the first three, so 'Jake' he was. A trifle corny, perhaps, but predictable.

We heaved a sigh of relief, as we drove into the fold-yard. The last few miles had been touch and go, with Jake becoming more active as the rope tying the sack grew looser. Anyway, here we were and the loose-box prepared for him had been carefully chosen. As well as opening off the calf-pens where we kept the goatlings, it also had another door on to the ings, where the ewes were grazing.

We'd always believed in putting new stock into a loose-box or pen of some kind for the first day, to give them a chance to settle in their

Jake – always belligerent.

new surroundings. In Jake's case, however, this was a mistake, as he made manifestly clear.

No sooner had Cyril removed the ropes, than Jake sprang from the sack in a quiver of rage. Once out, he vented his wrath upon it, bringing down his two front feet in mighty stamps on the offending sack.

"Now, now, old chap," said Cyril, placatingly, stretching his hand towards the enraged ram. If looks could have killed, Jake would have felled him, then and there. His whole attitude see.ne to yell a defiant "Don't you 'old chap' me!"

As it was, he lowered his head menacingly, presenting the four massive horns towards this presumptuous male human, and then reared up on his hind legs. I hurriedly backed towards the gate.

"Come out! Leave him to settle down," I urged.

Cyril reluctantly backed slowly away, closing and bolting the gate behind him. Then, climbing on, we leaned on the top rail, to observe how quickly he did indeed settle down.

Settle down? We would have been there yet; Jake never did settle down like the rest of our stock, most of whom actually seemed to be fond of us. His masculinity was always displayed in a challenging arrogance, and he was never really friendly towards us. Now, as we hurriedly left him to his own devices, he put on a show which, in a human being, would have been labelled a tantrum.

First of all, he set himself square, head down and horns towards us. This attitude was followed by several loud thumps of his front feet on the ground. Then followed a performance which left us speechless.

Jake began to circle the loose-box, getting faster and faster, while we watched, almost mesmerised. He careered round the loose-box, at ever-increasing speed, until he actually began to run up the walls like a rider on the 'Wall of Death,' so great was the propulsion. As his speed increased, he actually reached a height of about three feet, before descending once more to floor level.

Cyril and I were speechless, never having witnessed such a performance before. We were terrified that Jake would slip and break a leg, but he wasn't the one who came to grief, as he proved. Skidding to a stop, he changed his tactics completely, and suddenly hurled himself at the door on to the ings. Head down, he charged at it with full force, the point on his forehead where the four horns met hitting the door with a shuddering thwack.

"Goodness!" gasped Cyril. "He'll knock himself out!" and descended from his perch, ready to enter the loose-box.

"Don't!" I begged, clutching his arm. "You can't tackle him while he's in this state. He must have gone mad!"

Realising that a blow from the enraged sheep could result in a broken leg, Cyril decided to abandon the heroics and climbed back up the gate.

Although the door was thick and sturdy, it was no match for the repeated deluge of blows rained upon it. We were witnessing a true 'battering ram' in action. The noise was earsplitting as the horns met the wood. Though the door began to give, the blows seemed to have no damaging effect on the ram, who had now turned his temper on it. Under the onslaught, the door began to splinter and, finally, with a flick of his heels, Jake was through, leaving a gaping hole in the planks of the door.

Gingerly, we climbed down and, crossing the loose-box, peered round the remnants of the door, wondering where the berserk ram could have got to.

To our amazement, the transformation was incredible. There he stood, with his flock of three females, quietly grazing. A veritable Dr. Jekyll, whose Mr. Hyde seemed never to have existed.

93

Although the company of the ewes calmed Jake down, it was many months before he lost his belligerence towards us. Though they would come to Cyril's whistle to be fed with lamb-nuts, he, to begin with, stood just out of reach, tossing his horns in a threatening manner and obviously suspicious of our attempts to gain his confidence.

He always remained difficult to confine, his ability to jump being far greater than that of even the average 'Jacob.' When he did effect an escape, he usually sought out Billy who, of course, was tethered. Whether he fancied Billy's harem, or whether he suspected that Billy had designs on his ewes, we never knew. Whatever the reason, Jake and Billy were undoubtedly arch-enemies. The goat's immense size countered the fact that he was fastened up when Jake attacked, but the ensuing battles were terrifying.

Cyril's first intimation that Billy was under threat was a sound from him rather like the trumpeting of an enraged elephant. This was the signal for Cyril to sprint, as fast as he could, to separate the combatants.

Luckily, there were only two fights as, when he realised the enmity between the two, Cyril was extra vigilant. After the first encounter there was only one other time that they met, and this was when Billy was moved to a new pasture, out of Cyril's view. All in all, they were pretty well matched, and the sounds of battle alerted Cyril before any damage could be done to either. Jake, then, would be seized by the horns and dragged back protesting and struggling to his wives. After the second battle, we made certain that the goats were always tethered well downwind of Jake's pasture.

Joanna's lambing time arrived, and she presented us with two ram lambs.

"That's great!" said Cyril, in disappointment. "We could have done with more females to build up the herd. Three ewes aren't enough to keep him happy, anyway!"

This I took to be a hint that we were to look for more ewes, to extend our flock. After all, any more lambs born to our three ewes would be Jake's progeny, so we would need more, unrelated ewes.

That Jake's masculine pride and prowess were not satisfied by three mates was brought home to us before many months were past. Cyril went to the ings gate one Sunday morning, calling the sheep and rattling a few lamb nuts in a plastic container. Although they didn't need this extra sustenance, when the grass was in its full flush, it was a means of checking them each morning and evening. They were by now in the habit of coming to his call, to be given a handful of titbits, and he could see that they were all present and correct, so to speak.

On this particular morning, however, all were not present. Jake was conspicuous by his absence.

"Jake's missing," Cyril announced, when he returned to the house after his morning's round. "I'll go right round the ings first, and see if I can find where he's got out."

This was no easy matter. Unlike Joanna, whose breaching of the fence left clues, Jake was more likely to have sailed over, in a running jump. There were, luckily, usually pointers as to where he'd landed, in the form of flattened grass and broken twigs, on the other side. When Cyril returned from his reconnaissance, he was downcast.

"I think he's got over among next door's ewes," he remarked gloomily.

My heart sank. The part of next door's land which Jake had penetrated consisted of several interlinked fields, totalling between fifty and sixty acres.

However could Cyril find him? I wondered. Worse than this, the fields were occupied by about three hundred ewes, all ripe for mating.

Cyril trailed miserably down the road and explained the position, apologetically, to our neighbours.

"Bless you, don't worry!" consoled the brothers. "We shall be bringing that lot up in a few days. We'll bring him with them and let you have him back."

"That's not what's worrying me," explained Cyril. "I don't want him to get any of your Leicesters with lamb."

This sent them into gales of laughter.

"He's only young! We've got four mature Leicester tups in with those ewes, all above four years old," protested one brother. "Anyway, he's only eighteen months. Our rams won't let him near any of their ewes," continued his brother, confidently.

Remembering Jake's demolition of the loose-box door on the day we'd bought him, Cyril still had his misgivings. He felt that nothing would stand between Jake and his goal, if once he made up his mind, even four mature tups. The brothers had never seen him in action!

95

Still rather apprehensive, Cyril went to see if he could spot Jake. He didn't take much spotting. His black patches, and four horns, made him stand out among the Leicesters like a beacon on a dark night. It was, however, impossible for Cyril to separate him from the vast flock, no matter how he tried. Rather than lurking on the fringe, like the interloper he was, Jake stood proudly in the centre, surveying the ewes with a proprietory air, as though in his rightful place. He was eventually returned by the brothers, who regarded his escapade with amusement, treating it like the lapse of a naughty schoolboy.

With the coming of lambing time, however, they had to eat their words as they ruefully counted the number of their lambs which sported black patches; a memento of Jake's glorious truancy.

CHAPTER NINE

Like a lot of other facets of our lives, our venture into pig-keeping was not planned. It just 'came about.'

Faced with an embarrassment of goat's milk, we discussed how best to turn it to profit and decided that it could be used to fatten up a couple of pigs. Having reached the decision, we were immediately engulfed in a surge of excitement. We have always counted pigs among our favourite animals and indeed, to my mind, the holding of a rejected piglet for bottle-feeding is only surpassed by the nursing of a human baby. I consider that no other infant is as silky-skinned and soft as a baby pig, although there are many who would disagree with me, I know.

Now came the problem. We didn't wish to buy our weaners from the market. For one thing, we only wanted two, and it was usually necessary to buy a whole penful at auction. In addition, we wanted to see that they had been kept in good conditions, and had no wish to purchase stock which could have been chilled or in contact with infected pigs of any kind.

Our enquiries met with no success at first. It appeared that there was a dearth of pig-breeders in and around the village. However, on the following Saturday morning, details of our plight were confided to the butcher's wife when she called in for her usual cup of coffee while on her delivery round.

"You can't do better than young Handley in Seaton!" she exclaimed. "His pigs are really good stock."

Having taken down details of his address, we could hardly wait for her to go, so that we could telephone him and make arrangements to call and see what he had available. We were in for a shock; faced with building after building of sows, weaners, families, porkers and bacon pigs, our request for just two faded into rather humiliating insignificance. However, they were a grand, healthy-looking lot, well bedded down in clean straw so, from among the teeming hundreds, we made our choice of two good gilts — firm-bodied, long-backed and, in our eyes, beautiful. We had come prepared with a tea-chest in the back of the car, expecting to transport them in warmth and comfort to the cosy sty which we had prepared for them.

Alas for our hopes. Things had changed in the last thirty years, and we found that the powers-that-be demanded a document known as a 'Movement of Livestock Licence.' Viewing our blank faces with sympathy, our pig-keeping friend tactfully offered to arrange this and deliver the pigs later in the week. We had therefore to contain ourselves in patience and go home without the new additions to our little farm. I was determined to be sensible and not grow too fond of them so, in my mind, instead of giving them names, I decided to call them Pork and Bacon as, at this time, we intended this to be their future.

Once established our porcine protegées did well on a diet supplemented with goat's milk. As they grew, our thoughts dwelt longingly on home-cured ham and bacon. It was so long since we had tasted these succulent dishes, that we wondered whether they were indeed as delicious in reality as in memory. Cyril rehearsed the curing process, in conversation, over and over again. The nearer it got to pig-killing time, the more nervous he became.

His bacon and ham had been the stuff that dreams were made of, but could he have lost his expertise? After all, a lifetime had passed since his last efforts in that direction and, not only was there money at stake if he failed, but months of feeding, cleaning out and tending would be wasted, if the ham and bacon did not cure properly.

What would be needed? The salt-petre we could get at a chemist's, but what about the rock-salt? In our youth, every village store had stocked it, as every farmer and cottage pig-keeper had produced bacon. After fruitless enquiries in York, we eventually found an unlimited amount in a health-food shop in a small market town a few miles away. All was ready.

Now Cyril began to waver. 'Pork' had grown into a far better specimen than 'Bacon.' She was longer, stronger, and had no less than fourteen teats. With Cyril, the keeping of livestock had always been synonymous with breeding, whether it was rabbits, budgies, dogs, or what. If he kept them, he bred from them. Nowadays, I would pass the pig-sty and catch him stroking Pork and rubbing her back and sides until she lay down and rolled over, grunting in ecstasy. Once she was in that state of bliss, he rubbed her tummy, establishing a bond and gaining her confidence. He appeared to be counting those promising teats, almost as though he was afraid some may have dropped off during the night.

Years ago, in the heady days of our pig-breeding career, we had owned a prodigious breeder, one Woodmansey Queen Mary VIII, whose name was inscribed in the Advanced Register of Fecundity. Mary had been the proud possessor of sixteen teats. Now here was a gilt with fourteen — a worthy successor to Mary. Smiling to myself, I watched him surreptitiously. I agreed that with the benefit of a freezer, perhaps one pig would provide enough pork for the two of us. After all, two hams and two sides of bacon would keep us and our family in plenty. Of course, I agreed, tongue-in-cheek, Griselda was too fine a specimen to waste on food. Griselda indeed! Steely determination had flown out of the window. In addition to a new name, Griselda had acquired a new personality. We could now lavish on her all the affection we had held in check. 'Bacon' had no such luck. The farmer next door was a qualified butcher with a licensed slaughterhouse, which certainly eased the burden of 'pig-killing.'

How different from our youth when the local butcher came and slaughtered in any old available building. I well remember his horror when he caught sight of me in an advanced stage of pregnancy.

"Don't let the missus come out of the house," he begged. "The pig won't cure if a lady in the family-way sets eyes on it."

So, until it was all over, I was confined to the cottage, to ensure success. In sober middle-age, of course, the danger of this was non-existent. Poor old Bacon was collected in the Land-Rover and trailer, taken to the slaughterhouse, despatched with a humane-killer, and returned in the form of two large hams, two sides of bacon, and any amount of pork joints and 'cuttings.' At one time, anyone killing a pig provided pork for the whole village, but now, with the coming of the freezer, it meant a winter of plenty. The disposal of the joints and chops left the way clear for the curing of the hams and bacon, a task approached with trepidation.

The dairy at the Manor had a salting slab down each side. On these, the sides were placed, rind upwards, to drain for twenty-four hours. After this, they were turned over and lain on a thick layer of salt, after the rind had been rubbed with salt until it began to 'sweat.' This is where the saying 'sweating like a pig' originated, I believe. Although we had chosen November for the peak of our self-sufficiency programme, we were now beset by doubts. Was the weather sufficiently cold? A mild spell would be disastrous, but so would a frost.

The weather forecasts were listened to avidly. Each day the flesh was inspected closely to check that the curing was proceeding successfully. Where salt had impregnated the meat, thereby leaving bare patches, more was sprinkled on to ensure that the meat was kept covered. To obtain a better flavour, Cyril had mixed a small quantity of Demerara sugar with the salt.

After three weeks of anxious care, the process was seen to have been successful. The hams and the sides of bacon were taken outside and all the salt washed off with a hose-pipe. They were proudly lugged back to the dairy where they were hung from the rafters. We stood and surveyed them with pride, wondering how long it was since the beams had held such a prime load.

"We'll cut into it for Christmas, when the family come," I resolved. So the bacon hung, drying and gathering flavour, while the days passed. One day, in mid-December, Cyril came in from the afternoon milking.

"Christmas be blowed!" he exclaimed. "We're having some ham for tea today!" So saying, he went into the dairy with a carving knife. Half-an-hour later, we sat down to a feast fit for a king; a slice of succulent pink ham, eggs from our own hens, and home-baked bread. Gingerly, we tasted the first mouthful. Ambrosia! It wasn't too salty, and the flavour was perfect — well worth waiting for, over the weeks of anxiety.

We glanced at each other across the table and smiled blissfully, replete and satisfied; our feelings were a mixture of contentment and smugness. The ham-curing was far more successful than we had ever dared to hope. Cyril had lost none of his skill in that direction.

While he had been curing the ham and bacon, I had dealt with the rest of the largesse from the pig. One of the perks was the fat, the large leaves of pure white fat from the inside, and also all that which lay under the rind. This I cut into dice to be rendered down in relays in a large pan, to make lard. As the smell rose from the bubbling fat, it brought back memories of my childhood when my father was a butcher. Every Monday on my return from school, I was met with the same sickly smell of rendering lard. My mother had poured it into greaseproof bags, each embellished with my father's name, whereas now I had pressed into service the large bread pancheon. Into this I poured the lard which oozed out of the cubes of fat. When the last drop had been extracted, it left behind crispy, crunchy pork 'scratchings,' over which Cyril drooled. The following day I weighed up the lard into greaseproof paper parcels and found that there were ten pounds. I considered it to be worth the smell and bother. The 'cuttings' were gently stewed and made into brawn and pâté to store in the freezer. So the winter stretched ahead, with the promise of rare treats and gourmet meals.

'Bacon,' then, had met the fate for which she was intended. Griselda, by a quirk of nature, was now heading down a different road, destined to be the founder of our pig herd.

How fortunate it is that we can't foresee the future. Although we had envisaged Griselda's destiny as a natural, and predictable, succession of events: conception, pregnancy, labour and, the final triumph, a good family of healthy pigs, fate held in store not just a smack in the face, but a veritable rain of uppercuts.

The first stumbling block, like so many, was the result of our unfamiliarity with modern farming practice. Gone were the days when it was possible to hire or borrow the services of a boar from a more affluent neighbour. As we had already discovered, in order to control both Swine Fever and Swine Vesicular Disease, the authorities had made it illegal to move pigs from one farm to another, or from farm to market, without a licence. While appreciating the necessity of this, we could but sigh for the days when a good boar was used to service all the sows in the neighbourhood. For a time, we were stumped. Although we had been the proud possessors of boars in our youth, it was impractical to keep two pigs as a married couple, so to speak. To justify both his initial cost and his upkeep, a boar must preside over a harem.

Looking back, we seemed to be like babes struggling through a wood of ignorance. The two brothers at the next farm were ideal neighbours, always ready to help with advice or with the loan of an extra pair of hands or an implement which we didn't possess. They must, however, have had many a laugh at our expense, although now, as on many other occasions, they came up with the answer to our problem. Cyril had gone along one day to give them a hand with their sheep, and returned with the news which seemed to answer our prayers. To our amazement, we found that the Artificial Insemination Service had now been extended to include the pig fraternity. Not only that, but he had been supplied with the name and address of a pig farmer who used the service and could give full details.

Another obstacle had been surmounted! Eventually, the forms were despatched and back came the information that we had been registered as the owners of a herd. (A herd? Of one?) The package also included a catalogue of boars available. No mail-order catalogue could have brought more pleasure. We spent a satisfying evening poring over the lists of regal names: 'King David, Emperor Napoleon,' and many others, all of which symbolised majesty and greatness. No mere Percys and Toms were here. Evidently, the annals of history had been combed to choose names befitting these stars of the pig world. We perused and discussed the lists until late into the night, comparing details of their progeny, size of average litter, and quality of meat, until we were in a confusion of indecision. Having only one pig in our poke, we felt that it was of the utmost importance to choose the best for her. No match-maker weighed up the grooms available for a bride any more carefully than we did. At last, the choice was made. Griselda was due in season in about a fortnight, so no more could be done until the crucial date. We ringed the name of the chosen mate, and left the booklet open by the telephone.

Although the daily routine went on as usual, goats were milked and fed, eggs gathered and in-season nannies put to the billy-goat, Griselda now took priority. As her season drew nearer, each day at feeding time Cyril would press down on her back with all his weight on both hands. This was to simulate the weight of the boar, to see if she would stand for service. Predictably, she shifted uneasily from one foot to another or even moved away from the trough, until, one morning, Cyril rushed back to the house flushed with excitement.

"She's standing!" he grinned, and went to the telephone to ring up before the 9.30 deadline. The girl at the pig-breeding centre asked a few questions to confirm that the pig really was in season, and noted the name of the boar whose semen was required. After taking down directions as to how to reach our holding, she assured us that the inseminator would be with us after lunch.

Having been used to seeing the A.I. man inseminating the cows on Cyril's father's farm, I felt rather blasé about the whole thing. Consequently, I took no particular interest in the process and, in fact, didn't even go out to the pig-sty, believing, rightly or wrongly, that these things were better left to men. Although I was, at the time, quite happy to hear the details second-hand, I was to pay for my rather off-hand attitude, as later events were to prove. When I learned, however, what had taken place in the pig-sty, I was pleased that I hadn't been there, as I don't think I could have contained my

102

laughter. Upon entering the sty, the inseminator first took out an aerosol spray and surrounded Griselda with the pig equivalent of 'Chanel No. 5' — odour of boar. This was followed by the usual back-pressure, to assure himelf that she was indeed standing. Turning to Cyril, he casually said, "Sit on her back, will you?"

"What did you say?" my husband asked, thinking that he hadn't heard properly.

"Go on, sit on her back, as though you're riding a horse." Now, Cyril had never been a particularly keen horseman, and to be asked to ride a pig seemed to him the height of folly, if not lunacy. It was obvious that the inseminator was waiting for him to mount his steed, so, overcoming his doubts, he complied.

Tentatively, he put one leg over the gilt's back, and gradually lowered his full weight on to her. Although the last few weeks had seen the building up of a rapport between Cyril and Griselda, he felt distinctly uneasy at this turn of events. As it turned out, she bore him with no apparent discomfort and, indeed, surrounded by a mist of boar-scent, she seemed to enjoy her burden. Consequently, he remained in this undignified and rather precarious position, acting as a surrogate boar, for about ten minutes.

Griselda.

103

As he grew more confident, and Griselda seemed unlikely to toss him over her head, he glanced over his shoulder at intervals, to watch the proceedings. Although he only did so through idle curiosity, the fact that he had the sense to see as much as possible was to prove a blessing. However, ignorance is bliss, and, after offering the A.I. man a wash and a cup of tea, we bade him a cheery "Goodbye!" until the next time.

We could now put Griselda to the back of our minds for the next four months, and treat her as just an ordinary member of the animal family. As her time drew near, Cyril busied himself in preparing a farrowing sty, the pig equivalent of a maternity ward. At one end of a large pig-sty, he built a wall of bricks, leaving a small opening big enough to admit young pigs, but not an adult. Over this compartment he fixed an infra-red lamp which, together with plenty of straw for bedding, would provide a cosy crèche for the babies. This was not only a haven, where the piglets could avoid being crushed by the mother's bulk, but also, as they grow older and mixed feeding began, it would become their own snack bar. Although they could come out to suckle at feeding times, within the creep feed there would always be food available to them, where greedy Griselda could not reach it.

Meanwhile, the expectant mum grew to almost mammoth proportions, as we eagerly conjectured how many young she could be carrying inside her. However, the daily round of tending the other stock proceeded uneventfully until, one morning, Cyril returned to the house after his morning routine to announce that Griselda had milk. This was a sure sign of the onset of labour, so our morning's work was punctuated by frequent visits to the sty to assess progress.

Eventually, at about two o'clock, our anxious vigil was rewarded when the first piglet appeared. Normally, a sow gives birth to her litter with little trouble and no help. The young ones are so small in proportion to the mother's size that they usually slip out easily. We settled down, therefore, to keep an eye on her and count the piglets as they appeared. The first four came tumbling out in fairly rapid succession, and were transferred to the nursery unit, under the warm lamp, After that — nothing!

Could this be all? No, it certainly was not! Poor Griselda strained, huffed, puffed, and groaned, but all to no avail. Although we comforted her as best we could, rubbing her back and massaging her tummy, no more piglets appeared. She was obviously growing weaker and becoming exceedingly distressed. How much were the vet's fees? We agonised. Not that it mattered, of course. Griselda was suffering and we were incapable of helping. Cyril telephoned the vet, who arrived in what was, I suppose, record time. To us, however, anxiously keeping watch over the labouring sow, time crawled, punctuated only by her panting.

At the vet's appearance, our spirits rose. He exuded confidence and the very tone of his first words, "Now then, old girl, what's the trouble?" filled us with hope.

He quickly put on rubber gloves and apron, and settled down to work. His well-soaped hand and arm disappeared into Griselda and, eventually, two dead piglets were removed. I could have cried over the poor little bodies, and Cyril's face mirrored my emotion. The vet was certain that there were more to come and, certainly, things seemed to be on the move.

Another seven piglets were born with no difficulty, following one another quickly into the world. Proudly, we transferred them to where their siblings snuggled in the warmth while, with a deep sigh, Griselda stretched out for a well-deserved rest.

The vet left, accompanied by our heartfelt thanks, and we returned to the sty to check that the afterbirth had come away cleanly. We had one more task before we could go back to the house for a belated tea. We carefully transferred the eleven survivors to their mother, to satisfy ourselves that they were all capable of sucking, and that each could find its way back to the warmth and safety of the nursery quarters.

After what seemed an eternity, we tottered back to the house. Who on earth had called it the good life? we wondered, as we sank into comfortable chairs. I don't know whether we or Griselda felt most exhausted by the ordeal but, after consideration, we realised that the pride in the litter — Griselda's pride, as well as ours — outweighed everything else. It was, indeed, the Good Life.

Once the trauma of her labour was over, Griselda proved to be a good mother, and the litter did exceptionally well, fulfilling our hopes that supplementing their diet with goat's milk would bring them on to the weaning stage faster. We often spent time in the pig-sty watching Griselda's gentleness with her family, marvelling at the delicacy with which she lowered her bulk to lie down, ensuring that all the litter were safely out of the way, and no stray was trapped or

Griselda's first litter.

in danger of being crushed, as so often happens when pigs are kept in the old-fashioned way, as ours were.

However, before the young pigs were ready to be weaned, we received a letter which gave us food for thought. It was from the A.I. centre, announcing that it was no longer a viable proposition to send out inseminators. To keep down costs, members would, in future, ring up to order the required semen, go to collect it and perform the necessary duties themselves. Our eyes met! We felt both disquiet and consternation. This was an unforeseen snag — a calamity, even. If only I had gone out to watch the previous service, we would have felt more sure that we could cope. Cyril knew what to do, but wasn't certain that I was capable of helping. At least we had a couple of weeks for the problem to simmer before we need really face it.

Time moves on inexorably, of course, but now it passed with the speed of an express train. The A.I. centre had sent an address from which we obtained a catheter, accompanied by a list of instructions as to how to use it. Taking into account the fact that, surely, a professional A.I. operative must receive some training, this did seem to us to be rather inadequate preparation for the job.

Cyril picked up the catheter in its plastic bag, studied it pensively and then put it down, without a word. Picking it up myself, I considered it thoughtfully. It wasn't really as I'd imagined it would

106

be. That is not strictly true, though, because I can't say that I'd thought much about it. If anything, I'd expected a common or garden plastic tube, but this was threaded at one end with a very deep thread.

"Surely this can't be right? Have they sent the wrong thing?" I questioned.

"No-o," answered Cyril. "Read this lot!" passing over the instructions.

Carefully, I studied the leaflet.

"Insert the catheter and turn in an anticlockwise direction, until it locks," I read.

If we'd been worried about the process before, we were even more worried now. How I wished that I'd gone as a spectator when the professional performed it.

"I don't think we can do it," I stated flatly. I may say, here and now, that I do not easily throw in my hand. My philosophy is that, if somebody else can do something, we'll have a go. However, whichever of us did which part of the service, I couldn't see us being successful.

"Nonsense," said Cyril, with a horribly false show of confidence. "Of course we can do it."

We read and re-read the sheet and studied the diagrams, but were still not even sure that we could insert the catheter correctly, though nature seems to have no difficulty. We hadn't too much time to think about it though, as before we could say 'Pink Pigs,' Griselda was in season again, and the inevitability of the D.I.Y. insemination was upon us. Once more, we went through the routine of booking the semen, but, this time, there was no comforting reassurance of an expert coming to perform the deed. We were now faced with our moment of truth!

The address given to us on the telephone was that of a filling station, of all places. It seemed odd, but who were we to question? We set off immediately, in order to be back in plenty of time to do the insemination unhurriedly and with care.

This is what we told ourselves but, in reality, we wanted everything prepared, so that we could pluck up our courage and, once we felt able to tackle the job, we could go and get it over with nothing to delay it.

We had expected, upon arriving at the garage, to receive instructions on how to reach the Pig Breeding Centre. However, we were to be denied a glimpse of the august premises. Awaiting us at the end of the journey was a polystyrene box containing all we needed. Feeling rather let down, we returned to the car and began the return journey.

Usually, when travelling by car, Cyril and I sing. Our voices aren't good, but our repertoire is extensive, including as it does songs from our schooldays right up to fairly modern tunes. The return journey, however, was passed in silence; indeed, in gloom. The nearer we got to Storwood and the waiting Griselda, the less confident we became. We knew that there was no escape as we couldn't afford to miss this chance of getting her 'in pig.' To wait another three weeks would play havoc with our budget and, in any case, would only delay what had to be done.

Upon reaching home, therefore, we had a quick cup, and then, armed with the catheter and phial of semen, made our way to the pig-sty. Griselda heaved herself to her feet as we entered, no doubt expecting a titbit. The two parties approached each other, meeting in the centre of the sty. After placing his hand on her back to confirm for the umpteenth time that day that she would indeed stand, Cyril inserted one end of the catheter and, holding the other end aloft, mounted the sow.

There was, of necessity, a rather drastic change in tactics from the previous occasion. Lacking the presence of a trained A.I. operative, it was now necessary for Cyril to face backwards on the pig, in order to hold the tube in place. I was too intent on trying to match up the end of the catheter with the neck of the phial to make any comment, but the sight was rather reminiscent of a circus clown riding a mule. How true was the simile! No sooner was he in position, than all hell broke loose! Showing the whites of her eyes (I hadn't known pigs could!), Griselda was galvanised into action. Round and round the sty she teetered, reminding me of a stout lady in high-heeled shoes trying to run away from a mugger. Hanging grimly on to her tail with one hand, Cyril was shouting, "Whoa! Whoa!"

Whether this was to me, or to the pig, I was not sure. In any case, I was too busy keeping pace with them in order that none of the precious fluid should be spilt. The whole incident could not have lasted more than a few seconds, but a lifetime seemed to pass as the three of us whirled round and round the pig-sty in a wild Tarantella.

The end came abruptly. Griselda stopped dead in her tracks. Cyril flew through the air, his arms flailing like a windmill in a gale, and landed flat on his back in the gunge of the pig-sty floor. Fortunately, I had the presence of mind to jerk the phial upright, so saving what was left of the semen. On second thoughts, however, perhaps it was a reflex action on my part, as there hadn't really been time to think.

Groaning and smelling rather pungent, Cyril slowly rose to his feet, holding his back. He looked at Griselda and, from his expression, all affection for her had, at that moment, deserted him. He looked as though he could have killed her.

"Is there any left?" he asked, without any real hope. I held up the phial.

"About half," I replied. Leaving Griselda smirking triumphantly, we beat a retreat to consider our next plan of action.

Obviously, we thought, in our anxiety we had misjudged the timing, and she was not yet ready for service. This couldn't be the true reason for her behaviour, we then decided, as she had shown every sign of being in season. While Cyril bathed and changed, I washed out the catheter in clean water and hung it in the dairy to dry. I wasn't sure where to store the remaining semen. Should it be frozen? No, that would probably destroy its potency. What about the fridge? I wondered. When Cyril reappeared, infinitely more fragrant than when he'd gone up stairs, he disagreed with this suggestion. After all, he reasoned, when kept inside the boar, it wouldn't be particularly cold. In the end, we decided to replace the phial in its polystyrene box and place it in the dairy, which was the coolest room in the house.

Once this was done, we sat down to discuss our next move over the inevitable cup of coffee. We certainly couldn't afford to buy another supply of semen and, in any case, we felt that it would be humiliating to admit our failure. We could, of course, let the three weeks pass and ring up to say that the insemination had not held, thus entitling us to a free supply. Not only did this approach strike us as dishonest, but it would expose our handling of the job as inefficient. After all, when the A.I. man had performed the service, she had 'held' with no trouble.

We discussed the fiasco in detail and, eventually, decided not to wait until the next day for our second attempt. She had stood to the pressure on her back, so must really be in season. It followed, therefore, that it must have been the technique that was faulty. Again and again, Cyril mulled over what we'd done, comparing it with the A.I. man's visit. At last, with a look of determination, he jumped up.

"Come on," he said. "Let's have another go."

Once again, we entered the pig-sty, armed with the necessary apparatus. Griselda eyed us warily as we made our preparations, but appeared to have settled down and to be her normal placid self again.

At this second attempt, there was a slight re-arrangement of the stages of the process. While I uncorked the phial, Cyril threw one leg over Griselda's back and lowered himself until he straddled her, gradually placing the whole of his weight upon her. To our relief, she responded with calmness and composure. Cyril was right in his diagnosis; she required the weight on her back before the insertion of the catheter. Of necessity, he still mounted the sow back to front. Gripping with his knees, he leaned precariously over her tail, obviously nervous.

Just to sit astride a thirty-stone sow, with both hands occupied, is terrifying enough. Add to this the difficulties of trying to decide which is anticlockwise, when seated in a reverse position, and then turning the catheter, holding it at the correct angle, with any pressure coming forwards rather than away, and the whole business made the Rubik Cube look like a kindergarten toy. Later, he admitted that he'd felt the apprehension that the rider of a bucking bronco must in the seconds before his mount is released from the pen. His fears were groundless, however, and Griselda stood as though rooted to the ground until the phial was empty.

The relief was wonderful. We came out of the sty, laughing at our earlier escapade. If only it could have been captured on film, it would have made an hilarious comedy. Even today, when we recall that hair-raising chase, with the three of us cavorting round and round the pig-sty, we end up laughing until the tears come.

After three weeks of anxious waiting, there was no sign of her coming into season again, so our ham-fisted efforts had borne fruit — in more ways than one! We could notch up another triumph in our list of rather odd qualifications. We were now a successful Pig A.I. team, though what was the use of this expertise, we didn't really know. Although it wouldn't do anything for a job application form, it gave us a glow of satisfaction. One more hurdle had been surmounted, and we could relax until the next crisis was upon us.

CHAPTER TEN

Spring at Storwood was a delight. Memories of the grim winter faded as the ground became carpeted with snowdrops. Even the roadside verges were covered with masses of the dainty little flowers, and I wondered why I'd never even noticed them on my daily journeys past the manor, when we'd live in Cottingwith.

They were soon succeeded by the cheerful glow of daffodils, blooming in great drifts under the trees along the canalbank. These were the delicate, pale wild flowers which I so prefer to the large and rather vulgar 'King Alfred's'. When I say 'vulgar,' don't get me wrong! I'm very fond of King Alfred daffodils scattered here and there, but the great banks of them which now form solid splodges on the entrances and exits of most towns and villages do seem to me to be a bit overdone.

With the spring came our annual crop of kids. We were lucky in that most of our herd gave birth to twin nannies. Of course, this built up the herd and meant that each year more and more of our goats came into milk, making the job of milking every morning and evening a real burden on Cyril.

When we were first married, we had lived with Cyril's parents on an isolated farm. Soon after our return from honeymoon, my mother-in-law said: "I think you should learn to milk. If the machines ever break down, we shall need every pair of hands." As there was a large herd of Friesians, I could see the sense of this. It didn't instil any feelings of confidence in me, however, and I trailed into the cow-house, behind Cyril and his brother, feeling distinctly nervous.

I had already learnt how to fasten up the cows and put on the milking machines, so the sight of them struggling and barging against the door jambs in their efforts to reach the dairy nuts in the mangers, no longer filled me with fear.

Nonetheless, I remained at the far end of the building until all the cows were in their stalls, munching happily. When they were all tied up, I was led to my victim.

"Now," said Cyril, "Topsy's the easiest to hand milk." So saying, he seated himself on an old upturned bucket and sent a steady stream of milk frothing into the pail.

"Put your hands over mine, and feel what I do," he instructed.

111

Having established a rhythm, he went back to the rest of the herd, to the job of machine-milking, presumably expecting me to produce a full bucket by the time he returned.

As soon as his hands left the teats, the spurts of milk ceased. Try as I may, I couldn't manage to get one drop, no matter how hard I pulled. Topsy evidently sensed the change of manipulators. Turning round inquisitively, she licked the side of my face. Her tongue was very rough, and not particularly comfortable.

"Perhaps she likes me," I thought, changing my grip.

Whether or not she liked me that particular day, I never knew, but her dislike of me certainly grew during our relationship.

When Cyril came back, there wasn't a single drop more milk than when he'd left us.

"What's up?"

"Can she be dry?" I ventured.

"Move over," he grinned and, sitting down beside Topsy, he filled the milk pail with no apparent effort.

"Dry!" he teased, "You must be joking!"

Try as I may, I never did master the technique of milking. Day after day, I crouched down beside Topsy and handled her udders as though they were bell-ropes in a vestry. Grimly, I pulled on her teats until sweat poured from me and it seemed as though I'd pull her to her knees, even though she weighed about a thousand pounds.

We'd now reached the stage when I believed her to be deliberately withholding her milk. No matter how hard I tried, I never did get a drop. I tried the long, slow pull, the short, sharp tug, and all the variations in between, much to the amusement of my father-in-law, brother-in-law and husband, whose cross-talk act did nothing to boost my self-esteem.

When they finished milking, Cyril would come and, to my increasing chagrin, effortlessly fill the bucket up with a steady stream of creamy, frothy milk.

I now began to notice that if I entered a particular field where Topsy was grazing, she would stop munching and turn her head to watch me. The crunch came when, one day, seeing me in the far corner of a field, she began to advance.

Hurriedly, I turned and began to make for the gate. It looked a long way off, so I quickened my pace, glancing over my shoulder. Topsy had broken into a canter, or was it a trot? Whatever it was, it was certainly faster than a walk! Throwing self-control to the wind

112

and forgetting all I'd been taught about not showing fear in front of animals, I began to run.

To my consternation, so did Topsy!

Terror lent wings to my feet! I pounded across the field, my heart racing and lungs about to burst. As the gate hove into range, I put on a spurt. I hadn't done a gate-vault since I was at school, but this one would have brought words of praise from my gym mistress. I flew over the gate like an Olympic gymnast and landed on the other side in a panting, quivering heap.

When I recovered my breath, and peered through the bars, it was to see Topsy about two yards away, cropping a juicy morsel, as though that had been the only reason for her jog across the field. I was obviously beneath contempt, and she ignored me completely.

Luckily, nobody had witnessed the ignominy of my flight. When milking came, however, I told Cyril what had happened and, though he found the tale hilarious, he agreed that my ham-fisted efforts to learn the mystery of milking should stop, though more for Topsy's sake than mine, I presumed.

Nearly thirty years later, I was once more put to shame. This time by a two-year-old! Little Tammy was fascinated at milking time and, when only a toddler, used to crouch at the other side of the goats to Cyril, peering upwards to see where the milk came from.

"Can I do it, Grandad?" she'd plead. Eventually, Cyril gave in. After all, he could never remember not being able to milk, and had certainly milked a cow at the age of two.

Tammy was given instruction, as I had been, but, in her case, with success. She trailed round after Cyril, with her own little bucket and milking stool, and had her own pet goat, Daisy, whom she milked whenever she was visiting us. Her rhythm was perfect and she got a froth on the milk and even managed to strip Daisy completely, emptying her udder.

This was more than I could stand. I found it humiliating to be beaten by a toddler, and determined that, this time, I would master the skill.

Cyril didn't comment when, after helping him to bring in and fodder up the goats one tea-time, I brought a stool and bucket in from the dairy.

"I'm going to milk," I announced, a little defiantly.

He considered for a few moments.

"Don't try Annie," he advised, "her teats are short and hairy."

113

"Like Ernie Wise's legs," I thought. I looked at the assembled nannies contentedly pulling at their hay.

"I'll try on Dinah," I suggested. She was one of the pair of twins which had been our second purchase, after Tinkerbell. Practically all the rest of our herd were home produced.

Placing my stool beside Dinah, and my pail beneath her, I tentatively grasped her teats.

"Squeeze — don't pull," came Cyril's voice. It was difficult to go against instinct, which was to pull. However, I gently squeezed, nay, stroked, and to my delight milk streamed out. At first, my sense of direction was way out, and instead of landing in the bucket, the first jet sprayed my skirt.

Nothing daunted, and hoping that Cyril hadn't noticed, I wiped my clothes, took better aim, and soon had a steady rhythm of squirts landing in the bucket.

I could milk!

It was easy!

Gradually, the bucket was filled with milk and I was filled with pride.

Alas! It goeth before a fall! As I relaxed, and before I could pick up the bucket of milk to take it to the dairy, Dinah stepped forward, her rear foot entered the bucket, and kicked the lot into touch.

It was unbelievable that so much could happen so quickly, and that the small pail could apparently hold such a large amount of milk.

It whirled behind her, and, as I tried to grab it, I received most of the contents full in the face and all down my front. The startled goat bucked in alarm and this time her hoof sent the stool flying in the other direction, to hit the wall with a crack.

I rolled away from the flying hooves, before they came down on my head and, scrambling to my feet, did my best to soothe the old girl.

I felt near to tears. After all these years, my attempts at milking had been successful, only to have the results of my labours wasted.

However, I'd at last mastered the technique, and now felt that I could cope, should Cyril for any reason be absent at milking time. After all, I'd always have Tammy to help me!

My other resolution, made this springtime, was to learn to spin. I felt that producing clothes, as well as food, was in the true tradition of self-sufficiency. The added bonus was that I felt that sitting by a spinning-wheel, gently rocking one foot and producing your own yarn to order, was a soothing and therapeutic pastime.

There was a very active spinners' circle in the area, but I felt diffident at joining these experienced ladies as a mere beginner. Once I could do it, I told myself, then I'd go along and join. It was this pigheadedness which led to my first mistake.

As soon as we felt that we could afford it, off we went to buy a spinning wheel. No advice was sought, no books were consulted. I chose my machine by appearance only. Rejecting the horizontal spinning wheels because I considered they looked clumsy, I chose a little gem — an upright Shetland-type wheel.

"After all," I thought, "if I don't manage to spin, it will always be an attractive artifact in the house."

As I have said, this was a mistake. Had I only known, the horizontal wheels are far easier for the beginner. In my blissful ignorance, I watched with mounting excitement as Cyril removed the components from their cardboard box and, in no time at all, assembled the spinning wheel. That was the easy part!

Armed with the instruction manual, which we'd bought in the shop, I first identified the different parts: the maiden, the fliers, the spindle. I felt I'd never remember all the names and functions. Reading further, I found that later, I was advised to procure, or make, a lazy kate and a niddy-noddy!

Before moving to the country, I'd always associated spinning wheels with fairy tales, but this was beginning to sound like a nursery rhyme. Whatever next? I wondered.

I couldn't even surmount the first hurdle.

"Practice treadling the wheel," I read. Nothing to it. I sat before the machine, foot on the treadle, and began — or so I expected. It was now that I spotted a deficiency in my upbringing. My mother had never owned a treadle-sewing machine. Treadling was an art which had escaped me. Thankful that I was alone, I persevered, but with no luck. Every time the connecting rod, linking the treadle to the wheel, reached the peak of its movement, instead of going over and continuing the revolution, it jerked back and spun the other way.

Just as I was on the verge of despair, the wheel began to obey the treadle, and my foot moved rhythmically up and down, with the wheel under my control. I went clockwise. I went anti-clockwise. I stopped treadling and I started again. Not a lot to boast about, but a small success, I thought. After all, I hadn't any fleece as yet.

Oh, hadn't I? Just at that moment, Cyril appeared at the back door, clutching a fleece, bought from one of the members of the spinning circle.

"I thought this would do for you to practise on, until our own are sheared."

To our amazement, the unrolled fleece covered a great part of the floor. It seemed huge compared with the size of a sheep. Not only was it extensive, it was also dirty, full of thorns, grass-seeds (and worse!) — and stinking of lanolin.

All those films showing Shetlanders sitting in the sun and chatting while the yarn ran through their fingers, hadn't prepared me for the realities of spinning.

Gradually, we sorted the fleece according to the diagram and stored the different parts in labelled newspaper bundles.

I was now ready to spin in earnest, so it was back to the book.

"You will have to do two things at once: work the treadle which turns both the wheel and the whole spinning unit, while at the same time, feeding the wool evenly and rhythmically into the hole at the end of the spindle."

It sounded rather like the trick of patting the head while rubbing the tummy, which I'd mastered as a child. I wasn't as quick to master this technique.

I should, of course, have joined the group of spinners. I never did get going properly until one of them gave up a half day to give me some tuition. Then, at last, I was away. I had, by the way, discovered that nowhere on a spinning wheel is there anything sharp on which 'Sleeping Beauty' could have pricked her finger.

I'd be the first to admit that my first efforts were far from perfect. My yarn varied in thickness from rug wool size to thin string.

Despite this, I pressed on, finding that spinning was indeed a soothing pastime. At last my efforts resulted in sufficient spun wool to knit a jumper for Cyril. In due course, it was plied and washed. I did consider trying to dye it, but left this for a later date.

Although Cyril wore his jumper proudly, it was strictly kept for work. Perhaps it was something to do with the texture. Although in places it was thick and chunky, in others the thread was so delicate as to resemble lace.

When I happened to meet up one day with a member of the Spinners' Circle, she bore down on me.

"How's the spinning going, dear?" she enquired.

"Oh-er — all right," I answered, a little self-consciously. "I've knitted Cyril a homespun jumper."

She was obviously surprised at my progress.

"Good, good!" she praised.

"Well, it's not very good. It's rather lumpy and bumpy."

She raised one eyebrow and smiled down at me.

"We call it 'ethnic,' my dear," she corrected, as she sailed on her way.

CHAPTER ELEVEN

As the spring drifted into summer, the trees on the canalbank burgeoned into leaf, until our view of the water was screened by a mass of greenery. Now, my way along the bank when I went on my stick-gathering expeditions was blocked in places by festoons of dog-roses which drooped from the willow-trees and straggled between them. The daffodils which had covered the bank were over, their place having been taken by sprinkles of red and white campion.

Whenever I had time to spare, my favourite haunt was the utter peace of the canalbank. To reach my haven, I could not now take the direct route from the back gate, straight down the little valley and up on to the bank. The lowest point of the ings was now covered by masses of yellow flag irises, whose spear-like leaves were like a marching army with swords held aloft, through which I picked my way.

I have always been a person who needs periods of solitude and, although my excursions down to the canal were ostensibly to gather sticks for firewood, they were really to enjoy the silence, and recharge my batteries.

One day in the spring, when Cyril brought me home from school, he'd said, "Just come down by the canal a minute. I've something to show you."

Drawing me to a standstill, he silently pointed to a huge willow-tree, which leaned out at a low angle over the water. I could, at first, see nothing except the greyish-brown of the trunk. I crouched in the undergrowth beside him, wondering what I was supposed to see.

Then there was a movement in a hollow about a yard and a half up the trunk. It was a mallard. She had made her nest and was now sitting on her clutch of eggs, well above the ground. We never knew what had caused her to choose this unlikely spot, rather than the reeds which fringed the water, but Cyril later approached the nest when she was away from it, and counted about sixteen eggs. We didn't disturb her, keeping well out of sight until, one day, the nest was empty. She and her brood had returned to the water.

When she had gone, her chosen willow became my vantage point. I could scramble along the massive trunk and lie in complete safety, looking down upon the canal.

Here, in the warmth of early summer, I would spend what time

118

Cyril and I viewing the willows along the canal.

I could spare stretched out along the trunk, watching the activity below me. I was fascinated by the flashes of the brilliant peacock-blue dragonflies, which darted among the reeds and rushes. The canal water-lilies were not the huge creamy or pink ones which grace the lakes of town parks, but smaller and deep yellow, almost as bright as the kingcups which grew on the bank. Among the stems I would sometimes catch a glimpse of a predatory pike, lurking in wait for his prey.

Sometimes, though not very often I must admit, the tranquillity was broken by the chug of a cabin cruiser, and I would watch it go by from my secret look-out. At first, I resented their presence, especially the calling from one passenger to another as they opened the little swing-bridge which spanned the canal further up. Later I decided that, even though they disturbed the wildlife, causing the ducks to squawk and flutter and the busy little coots and water-hens to scurry for the shelter of the reeds, they had a right to share the pleasures of 'our' canal.

I often wondered why I'd been so reluctant to move to Storwood. The discomforts of winter were pushed out of my mind and it now seemed like an earthly paradise, each day bringing new discoveries to delight us.

In addition, of course, each day brought its share of hard work and problems. Earlier in the year, we had decided to save the ings grass for hay and so had moved the sheep into Blackgates field, which had been occupied by the goats. The goatlings and kids were tethered on the wide grass verge opposite the house but, each morning after milking, Cyril staked out the Billy and the nannies on the opposite bank of the canal.

This added considerably to his work-load, especially on the days I was at school in York. It necessitated two or three journeys along the dirt track which divided our land in two, and led to Tim's house. From here, the path went through the garden in front of his house and over the small swing-bridge, to the other side of the water.

Although most of the adult goats were placid in their maturity, Tim was a keen gardener. The path through his land was a public right-of-way, to be sure, but was used only occasionally by fishermen. Cyril, therefore, needed all his wits about him on his daily journeys to ensure that no goat was able to indulge in a snack snatched from Tim's immaculate rows of vegetables. He preferred to take only a few at a time and do an extra journey than upset our neighbour.

The bridge was also an added obstacle. None of the goats ever became used to hearing their hooves resounding on its metal surface, and needed patient urging before they would reluctantly cross. Once over, his task wasn't too difficult. He'd usually been down beforehand and moved the stakes, so it was just a case of dropping each chain over a stake, as he passed on to the next.

Griselda was, by now, well into her time with her second litter. We became more excited as her farrowing date drew near, feeling that we'd been involved from the word 'go.'

Consequently, when one day Cyril called to pick me up at home-time with the words "Come on! Hurry up! Griselda's got milk!" I felt just as excited and, indeed, as tense as he appeared to be. As the car pulled up in the fold-yard, we were out almost before it stopped, looking anxiously over the pig-sty door.

"Good, she's started," Cyril commented. "At least it's not a bed-time job."

"Are there only the two up to now?" I queried, as he went inside and moved the two piglets under the infra-red lamp.

"Yes and what's more they've been born quite a while. She's licked them clean and they've had a feed."

"Oh dear. I hope there are some more to come," I ventured, remembering many years ago a single piglet, Primrose, who grew as round as a barrel, being the sole recipient of her mother's milk.

"Of course there are!" scoffed Cyril. "Look at the size of her." Lying on her side in the straw, Griselda did, in fact, look more like a grounded barrage-balloon than a sow. We waited for a few moments and then, there being no sign of any more young emerging in the immediate future, we went into the house for tea.

This was, of course, a hurried affair, no sooner eaten than we were out to the pig-sty in quick-sticks. To our disquiet, though Griselda was still in labour, there was no sign of any more babies.

"Oh, no," Cyril groaned. "Don't tell me we're going to have a performance like last time!"

He went in and inspected the sow and the surrounding bedding. There was no sign of the afterbirth, so she evidently hadn't finished her labour.

"Go and ring the vet, love. I'm not having her suffering like she did before." Cyril looked quite desperate.

Quickly, I returned to the house, only to meet with a sickening disappointment.

"I'm sorry, Mr. Wood has just gone out on a case. I'll get in touch with him, but I can't say how long he'll be."

Thanking the receptionist, I put down the telephone and returned to the sty. I knew that Cyril was worried, and, as he knew more about pigs than I did, I felt there was just cause for me to worry as well.

As I entered, I could see that Griselda was becoming distressed. Her body was heaving and, as Cyril crouched over her, he turned to me.

"Well?"

"He can't come yet. He's out on a case."

His face fell.

"There's nothing else for it. I must do the best I can," he muttered grimly. "Come on, love."

With this statement he leapt to his feet and brushed past me on his way to the house. I had to run to keep up with his determined strides.

"What are you going to do?" I gasped breathlessly, hurrying beside him.

"I must do what I can to help her, I'm going to bring them."

"But you can't! How do you know what to do?"

"I've calved plenty of cows. It must be the same only on a smaller scale," he replied, as he went to the kitchen sink and began to wash his hands, scrubbing his nails with ferocity. I didn't really know what to think of this turn of events.

"Where are your rubber gloves?" he demanded.

"Under the sink, but will they fit you?"

While he was drying his hands and arms, I ran up the back stairs for talcum powder. By the time I returned, he was washing the rubber gloves. Luckily, Cyril has quite small hands for a man and, with a liberal sprinkling of talc, he managed to force his hands into the gloves.

He stripped to the waist and commanded: "Bring me a clean bucket of hot water, soap and a towel," and hurried from the kitchen.

My mind was in a whirl, but I did as ordered and shot out after him, carrying my load. I even stopped to put a dash of antiseptic in the water, for which I gave myself a mental pat on the back.

When I reached the sty, Cyril was already stretched out on the straw. Motioning where he required the bucket to be placed, he dunked his hand and arm in, and then liberally soaped them. When I began to make a remark, he ignored me and gently inserted his well-soaped arm into the panting pig.

"Well!" I thought, "now I'm taking second place to a sow!"

With a look of concentration, Cyril groped inside the straining pig. "Now, now, old girl," he soothed, "Just take it easy."

I couldn't believe that Griselda was once again having difficulty farrowing. Perhaps there was something wrong with her insides, I thought.

Cyril suddenly gave a grunt, twisted his arm and withdrew it, gently bringing out a piglet. "There, that's out!" he gasped. The dead piglet was about twice the normal size, bloated and swollen. Cyril sat back on his heels, mopping his brow with his forearm. "I wonder if that's all that's wrong," he questioned.

He washed his hands and arms, removed the rubber gloves and, after drying himself, put on the shirt I'd brought along. "I think this little joker was blocking the way," he offered, "Or, at least, I hope so."

So saying, he crouched down again and we settled down to await any further developments. We hadn't long to wait. One by one the

122

piglets came tumbling out into the world, until we had transferred no less than thirteen to the nursery unit. That was, of course, including the first two. They were all good pigs, no runts nor wrecklings.

Heaving a sigh of relief, Cyril said, "Go and ring the vet. We shan't need him now. I'll just stay until she cleanses." This was the farming term for the coming of the afterbirth.

As I reached the door, he called, "Hey!"

I turned to see him smiling. So great was his relief that his face would have put the Cheshire cat to shame.

"Put the kettle on, love, I could do with a cuppa."

It was the story of our lives, I thought, as I put the kettle on the stove. Every crisis was alleviated by the ubiquitous cup of coffee.

A few weeks later, a visitor to the farm leaned on the pig-sty door and gazed at Griselda, lying in the straw, with her litter of thirteen piglets, each attached to a teat, sucking and gurgling noisily over their feed.

"What swine's responsible for that lot?" he queried, cockily.

"Well, actually, I am," Cyril answered, winking at me.

To say that the visitor was dumbfounded is to put it mildly. He looked from one to the other of us, wondering what on earth Cyril meant. At last, Cyril explained that from conception to delivery he'd been, more or less, responsible for the litter, and felt justifiably proud of them.

Cyril's enforced duties as midwife to Griselda had saved the vet's fees, to be sure, but we knew better than to try to usurp his skills. So it was that, not many days later, we had to call upon his services again.

The in-milk nannies slept in what had originally been a calf-house. At one end of this was the large loose-box where we had tried to contain Jake on his arrival. The rest of the building was divided into ten very sturdy pens, with strong wooden walls and secure doors. Each goat knew her own compartment, and would go to it unhesitatingly, when they went in for the night.

Each morning, when Cyril unbolted the outer door and went down the central corridor, rattling his containers of dairy nuts, the nannies would jump up, forelegs resting on the doors or partitions to watch his progress. Although he was as quick as possible in doling out the rations, those who were not first-served would bleat their complaints, until he reached them. They obviously waited with

123

eagerness for his arrival, which was heralded with excitement and affection — cupboard love? Not entirely.

One particular morning, when the nannies hung over their doors to watch his progress, there was one exception — Annie (she of the short, hairy teats). Cyril fed the others and then, before leading any of them out to the milking parlour, went into Annie's box.

He was perturbed to find her still lying down.

"Come on, old lass," he urged, trying to raise her to her feet. He was eventually successful, but she stood with her head down, ignoring the dairy nuts, which he rattled enticingly before her. Her eyes were lack-lustre, her coat dull and lifeless and, though he could see nothing obviously wrong, she had the withdrawn look of a sick animal.

Before beginning the milking, Cyril went back to the house to 'phone the vet. This time, he was more fortunate and was promised an immediate visit. He had only just finished cooling the milk when the vet's car pulled into the yard.

"Now, Mr. Sunley, you've got a sick goat, I believe," as he opened the boot and took out his case. He was a large young man, fresh-faced, with a luxuriant black beard, who exuded confidence and reassurance.

When they went into Annie's stall, she was once more lying prostrate.

"Come on, Annie," Cyril cajoled. "Up you get, lass."

At last, she rose unwillingly to her feet, but stood downcast, as before.

"Mmm! She certainly isn't at all well," observed the vet.

"What an understatement!" Cyril thought.

However, he couldn't complain at the examination of Annie. Her temperature was taken, her eyes peered into with a torch, her head was felt between the base of her horns and she was gone over very thoroughly with the stethoscope.

"I'm afraid it's pneumonia," was the verdict.

"She seemed as right as rain yesterday," said Cyril, "I can't understand it. She's not been in a draught, nor treated any differently than the others."

The young vet felt her udder.

"You'll find she's dry," he announced. "I'll give her an injection and come again tomorrow. Meanwhile, keep her warm."

With that, he was on his way. Cyril brought out the coat which

124

had been first made for Billy and fastened it round Annie. He then left her to sleep, as she appeared to be drowsy.

When he went in about an hour later to check the goat, Cyril was amazed to find her on her feet, looking alert and obviously hungry. He couldn't believe the improvement, it was so dramatic.

Had the vet discovered the Elixir of life? he wondered. He filled Annie's hay net, so that she'd have some to pull at, not only as food, but also to keep her occupied while she was alone. Boredom is just as bad for animals as it is for people, we believe.

The vet was obviously delighted with Annie's progress when he returned the next day. Notwithstanding, he gave her another thorough examination. "That's more like it, old girl, isn't it?" he murmured sympathetically. He administered a second injection and then turned to Cyril. "There, Mr. Sunley. She should improve from now on. Don't put her out for a week or so, except when it's very warm." He rubbed her horns in a farewell gesture, as he strode out to continue his rounds.

Annie certainly did improve by leaps and bounds. Although she didn't regain her milk, her appetite returned and it wasn't long before she was going down on the sheltered canalbank, with the rest of the herd.

It came, therefore, as a terrible shock when, one morning about three weeks later, Cyril went to the calf-pens to find Annie lying dead in her stall. She'd seemed perfectly fit and well when he'd checked the stock at bedtime the previous night, and her death remained a mystery.

Our only explanation was our belief that goats are not tough animals and even a comparatively mild shock can cause a deterioration in their condition, even, it appeared, death. In the end, we decided that her heart had probably been weakened by the bout of pneumonia and that she'd died of a heart-attack.

I suppose even Paradise must have its off-days. Certainly when it's an earthly one, it does. When dealing with nature, whether animals or plants, one can never sit back and feel complacent. We found that whenever things seemed to be going well, there was usually a sock in the solar-plexus waiting to be delivered. As Cyril was fond of saying: at least it kept us on our toes.

125

Before long, we felt that our spell of bad luck was, perhaps, over. A few days after the death of poor Annie, Cyril received a visit from a nearby farmer. He was a man not particularly well-known to us, as his actual farm was in a village a couple of miles away. His land, however, stretched over to the swing-bridge which crossed the canal, almost reaching ours.

"Now, Ci-rill," he began. "Aa've noticed your sheep're peeling t'grass off yon little field. Aa'm moving marn into t'field by t'beck, and wondered if you'd like ti put yours in wi' 'em for a while, ti give your grass a chance ti grow a bit."

Cyril couldn't believe his ears. It was true that the sheep were becoming a worry to us.

In order to keep the ings land for hay, they'd been moved into a little paddock which was proving too small to sustain them without additional feed.

Consequently, Cyril thanked him profusely.

"Aa'll let yer know when Aa puts marn in, then thoo can move yourn," said our benefactor, and away he went.

When Cyril came into the house, he was full of praise for this neighbourly act.

"I hardly know old Arnold Jones," he admitted, "and yet he's offered me free grazing for a few weeks."

"Are you sure he doesn't expect us to pay?" I enquired, having learned the meaning of the word 'agistment' when I was first married. This is an arrangement whereby one farmer pays another to allow animals to graze on his land.

"No-o. He didn't mention money. I think a lot of the farmers feel sorry for us," said Cyril. "They think we've a screw loose."

"They certainly think we're a bit eccentric," I said thoughtfully, "though I can't for the life of me think why."

The offer of free grazing slipped from my mind as I prepared for the coming visit of Paula, Clive, toddler Imogen, and Verien, the baby. In my excitement at the thought of seeing them and the excess of cleaning and baking which occupied me, I thought no more about Mr. Jones's kind gesture.

When he walked into the yard a few days later and stood, leaning on his shepherd's crook calling, "Ci-rill, Ci-rill!" I remembered his

126

offer and went out to greet him.

"Is t'maister in, missis?" he asked.

"Yes, he's somewhere about," I answered, adding my voice to his.

We must have raised a loud chorus, as Cyril came round the end of the barn, red-faced and panting. He'd obviously run some distance, expecting an emergency.

"Yes?" he asked, looking from one to the other.

"You can move them sheep wheniver you want. Mine's in."

"Thank you," we said together, but it was unheeded, as he strode purposefully out of the fold-yard, looking somewhat Biblical with his crook.

"I certainly want to move them, but it's a bit of a problem," Cyril said.

"Why?"

"Well, it's not like taking the goats down. I don't fancy trying to herd six sheep through Tim's garden," he explained. I could see his reluctance. Sheep wouldn't take kindly to being caught, tethered, and put on leash, like goats. It was alien to their nature. They hadn't been reared that way.

The thought of Jake running amuck through Tim's garden was enough to make a strong man (or woman) quail. I thought of the hours our neighbour wielded his hoe, and my heart sank.

"Let's wait until Paula and Clive come at the weekend," I suggested. "The more of us there are, the better."

"That's a good idea," said Cyril, with relief, and so the evil day was postponed.

When Paula and Clive arrived, with their little family, we let them settle in on the Saturday, before breaking the news of what was required of them on Sunday morning. They were, of course, full of enthusiasm. I find most people are, when faced with the chance of farmwork. I must admit that we, too, find it fun. So it was that, after Sunday morning's milking and the staking out of the goats, we all armed ourselves with sticks, and set off for Blackgates field. Even two-year-old Imogen had her little jeans tucked into mini-wellies and brandished a garden cane.

The sticks, of course, were not to be used to hit the sheep; they were merely an extension of the arm, in case one of the herd turned the wrong way and needed to be ushered back to its proper path.

Of course, the sheep were at the very bottom of the field. It's typical of animals that they're usually in the wrong place. I've noticed, when we come to move stock, that there's never a short, nor easy, way.

Paula had strapped Verien to her body, in what's known as a sling. I found this a weird and wonderful contraption but must admit that they're very convenient and, certainly, the infants appear contented when slung close to their mother. I wasn't too happy on this particular occasion to see one of my grandchildren bumping about when her mother intended to herd sheep, no matter how small the herd. However, needs must, when the devil drives.

First of all, Cyril propped open the gate. Then, accompanied by Imogen, who strode beside him in a very determined fashion, he worked his way to the bottom corner of the field to get the sheep on the move. The whole proceedings, of necessity, were conducted in slow motion. Once the little flock became excited, all would be lost, and the job could take twice as long.

Slowly, he ushered them up the hill towards the gate, moving from one side of the group to the other, arms outstretched and constantly talking to them in a soothing voice. Clive had gone down the little lane, where the gate to Tim's garden stood wide open. Paula was in the lane, as it led to the main road, to stop them going the wrong way, while I stood in the gateway of the stackyard field, which we'd made into our vegetable garden.

We'd always meant to put a gate on this field, but had never got round to it, there being always a more urgent job to be dealt with. Now, as I stood with arms and stick held sideways, I could not, for the life of me, recall any job that had been more urgent than that particular one.

Suddenly, they came over the brow of the hill, heading for the gate. They were moving briskly, but not running and were certainly well under control. At the gate, there was a small hesitation, while their eyes darted from side to side, wondering which way to go. I moved forwards into the lane and waved my left hand, to turn them down towards Tim's house. As though with communal mind, they swung round and headed towards Clive, who was waiting about a hundred yards away. Pushing Imogen through the gate, with the instruction "Follow the sheep," Cyril swung the gate shut and began to hurry down the field-side of the hedge, knowing that there was a spot at the end where he could climb over a short piece of fence and join Clive, hopefully before the sheep reached the spot.

Breathing a sigh of relief that they were all moving down the lane,

128

I moved forward to follow them, in order to be close behind as they passed through Tim's garden.

My relief was premature!

I don't know whether it was the slam of the gate closing which startled him but Jasper, the last one through, was galvanised into action. Looking wildly both ways, he suddenly decided, in a most un-sheeplike fashion, not to follow the herd. Instead, he turned the other way, and headed for the main road.

"Look out, Paula!"

I will admit that she stood her ground until the last possible moment but, even when faced with waving arms and stick, Jasper seemed to have no intention of stopping.

"Turn him! Turn him!" I yelled, but as he approached her, she clutched the baby and jumped out of the way.

"Oh, goodness knows where he'll end up!" I groaned. "Follow the others and give your dad a hand, will you?"

So saying, I broke into a run, following the fleeing lamb. When I reached the house, I stood, undecided, in the road at the point of the right-angle. "Now," I wondered, "which way is he likely to have gone?"

Before I came to a decision, I heard voices round the bend in the road which led to Cottingwith. Then Jasper appeared round the corner, being ushered along by three old gentlemen from the village. Their gentle Sunday morning stroll brought them past the manor every week. This Sunday, their timing was perfect. They spread across the narrow lane, arms stretched sideways, ambling along, with no break in their conversation, nor alteration in their pace. Nevertheless, they'd checked Jasper's headlong flight, and were now guiding him back with the apparent ease of experts.

I took my place in the centre of the lane, on the other arm of the right-angle, hoping that my outstretched arms would provide as big a deterrent to the errant sheep as theirs had done. He only hesitated for a second, and then at a brisk trot set off down the cart-track.

"Thank you so much," I panted, as I set off in pursuit. I knew I was supposed to gentle him along at an unhurried pace, but he was the one who was running. I was merely keeping him in sight.

Down the slope through Tim's garden we sped and, as Jasper headed for the swing-bridge, I was thankful to see that the rest of the sheep were in the field with Arnold Jones's flock.

At the far side of the bridge, the canalbank was roughty ten yards wide, running to the north and south. This tow-path was bounded on the west side by a steep-sided beck, which was, in effect, a land-drain. Mr. Jones's field was at the other side of the beck, reached across a brick culvert, which the years had covered with grass, so that it was indistinguishable from the surrounding land.

As we jogged down the steep path, which bisected Tim's garden, I noted that Cyril was standing by the field-gate, one hand on the latch to swing it open upon Jasper's approach. Paula and Clive were stationed at the far end of the bridge, poised like goalkeepers, ready to dart sideways to keep Jasper from the towpath.

His speed had by now slowed considerably, for which I felt thankful, as I slackened my own pace, to catch my breath. At last I felt that I could relax. Do I never learn?

As soon as he heard his hooves on the metal bridge, Jasper was spurred once again into activity. He dashed across and jerked to a sudden halt, as he spotted Cyril waiting ahead. He paused long enough to glance right and left and see that his flight along the towpath was apparently blocked.

Who said sheep were dumb?

Jasper noticed an escape route which we'd missed.

Clive's side of the bank was partially blocked by a tree-trunk, washed down by the floods and deposited there when they receded. Although we'd noted the tree's immense girth and relied upon it to block his way. To our amazement, Jasper soared over it with ease and was left teetering on the narrow ledge between the trunk and the beck.

We stood rooted to our posts, unable to believe what had happened. Cyril left the gate, crossed the culvert and began to walk along the towpath at the other side of the trunk, intending to go and corner the lamb.

We closed in, confidently expecting this to be the job of a moment, presuming we were merely to be needed as back-up, in the unlikely event of Jasper evading Cyril's grasp. I should have known better than think we could anticipate an animal's next move.

We were poised for a recapture when, from the other side of the beck, Joanna spotted her wayward lamb. With a bleat of recognition, she ran across the field, followed by the rest of our little flock. They lined the bank, baa-ing in chorus, to greet their missing member.

These friendly faces and welcoming voices were too much for

Jasper. To the accompaniment of their cheers, he launched himself into the air, determined to leap the beck, like an ovine Evel Knievel. He failed, of course! Instead of landing on his target, he plummeted into the beck below. To our consternation, Cyril leapt after him, disappearing from our view down into the eight-foot drop.

My heart was in my mouth as we dashed forward and peered over. There, well below, were Cyril and Jasper, locked in what appeared to be mortal combat. There was as much mud in the beck as water, and both my husband and his captive were coated in the stuff.

"There!" exclaimed Cyril, glowering at the lamb. "Gotcha!"

Thus saying, he grasped him firmly round the middle and dragged him to the side. As he looked up, and we looked down, it was obvious to all of us that there was no way he was going to scale the steep side, heaving the struggling lamb.

"Come down and give me a hand," he begged.

Now that we knew that both he and Jasper were unhurt, we were rather reluctant to join them. There was no alternative, of course. We joined hands to make a chain and drew them up the bank.

What a bedraggled pair they looked, as we dragged them up. Both were drenched and their legs were encased in mud, giving both beast and man the impression of wearing black stockings. When he reached the bank top, Cyril gave Jasper a push to rejoin his family and then threw himself down on the grass, a picture of dejection and exhaustion.

"I wonder if there's some way I could buy his clothes wholesale?" I pondered, as I looked down at the sorry-looking object at my feet. On second thoughts, perhaps I should patronise the local jumble-sales and savour the sartorial delights on display there.

When my raggle-taggle of a husband rose slowly to his feet, I found I couldn't meet his eyes, in case he noticed the laughter lurking in mine. With poker faces, avoiding looking at each other, we set off back across the swing-bridge, Cyril squelching at every step.

Suddenly, our silence was broken by Imogen's announcement, to the world in general: "Grandad all wet!"

"Yes, darling," I answered, and then caught Paula's eye.

We couldn't contain ourselves any longer and even Cyril joined in.

"Whatever do I look like?" he spluttered, wiping his eyes.

131

I couldn't really reply. Visions of King Neptune crossed my mind as I looked at his wet clothing, mud-bespattered face, caked legs and the trails of pond, or river, weed hanging from his pockets and clinging to his clothes. "Anyway," he continued, when the laughter died down. "At least we've moved them and they're knee-deep in grass."

Our guests didn't realised what a relief it was for our little flock to be moved from our own pasture. However, the saga wasn't yet ended.

A day or two later, we received yet another visit from Mr. Jones. When I saw him approaching, I couldn't believe my eyes. Three visits in just over a week, when he'd never done us the honour before! However, when Cyril went to greet him, all was revealed.

"Aa'm tekkin t'missus away for a week. Can you keep your eye on't sheep?"

"Of course," answered Cyril, in full realisation of the fact that we were in his debt. As he turned from the door, he paused. "There's a bucket by t'trough. I fill it from t'beck, every day."

When he returned to the breakfast room, Cyril's face was a study.

"The old rogue!" he exclaimed.

"Why, what's wrong?" I asked.

"I wondered why he'd made such a kind offer, when we hardly knew him," he grinned ruefully, and went on to explain.

"Anyway," he continued. "It's a small price to pay for all that grass."

He changed his tune, however, upon going down next morning to check the sheep. The horse-trough, which stood up on the bank of the beck, was completely dry. Looking round, Cyril saw a plastic bucket with a length of rope attached to the handle.

It was a hot sunny morning, and he'd no pressing work waiting at home, where the milking, feeding and tethering out had been finished before he had gone down to the pasture.

Consequently, it was with a feeling of lightheartedness that he dropped the bucket down into the water. It was unexpectedly heavy when he hauled it up, but not sufficiently to cause unease. Whistling to himself, he walked the couple of steps to the trough and sloshed the water in.

Now he did begin to feel uneasy. The bucketful had only more or less moistened the bottom. In addition, the sound of the water sploshing had acted as a signal to the thirsty sheep. Calling to one

132

another, they cantered from all corners of the field, surrounding both Cyril and the trough.

Now he had to push his way through them to the brink of the bank each time he filled the bucket. Each time, of course, the bucket felt heavier and, at first, the sheep devoured the water as fast as he put it in. When had old Arnold Jones last filled it up? he began to ask himself.

As the sun rose, and beat down more relentlessly, he discarded his shirt and the sweat ran down his body. He pushed the sheep out of the way and tried to speed up the process.

Gradually, the sheep drifted away across the field, as their thirst was assuaged. Cyril gritted his teeth and forced his aching arms and shoulders to carry on, determined to leave the water-trough brimful when he went back to the manor. It was almost too much, but he grimly carried on. When, eventually, the trough was as full as possible, he made his way slowly home. The 'little' job had taken him most of the morning.

When he picked me up in York, he poured out the whole tale. His shoulders ached so much that even steering the car was painful.

When the other stock had been dealt with after tea, we took a second plastic bucket and a piece of rope with us, when we strolled down to check the sheep.

"If we can top it up tonight, they won't drink once it gets dusk, and then it'll make the job easier in the morning," Cyril decided.

To our relief, the trough was only about half-empty.

"We'll take it in turns," I suggested, tying the rope on to the handle of the second bucket.

"You'll never manage it, love," he protested, but I was determined to pull my weight He was right! After the fourth or fifth bucketful, I felt as though my arms and shoulder joints were on fire. I could feel that my face was glowing like a beacon with the effort of dragging the full bucket up the bank.

"Leave it," ordered my lord and master, "I'm not having you knocking yourself up."

I felt both frustrated and humiliated, but was forced to admit that he was right. We compromised. Cyril knelt on the bank and drew up the buckets and I carried them and emptied them into the trough. This saved him the effort of getting up and walking, and having two buckets made it a smooth operation.

Predictably, the week of old Arnold's holiday was the hottest of the summer. Consequently, not only did the sheep drink more, but Cyril's efforts were conducted in simmering heat. By the end of the week, however, his muscles and joints had become used to the task and he found it easier. Perhaps the fact that the great majority of the sheep belonged to somebody else had made him more conscientious, but I'm sure the trough was never normally kept so full.

At the end of the week, Arnold Jones once more strode into our fold-yard.

"Ci-rill!" he yelled.

Cyril popped out of one of the buildings, a relieved smile wreathing his face.

"Aa'm back!" announced Arnold rather unnecessarily. "Everything all right?"

"Yes, of course — no trouble at all," lied my husband (not bothering to tell of the morning he'd gone down and found both herds missing, which had entailed half a day's work to round them up!)

"Good," he answered laconically, and went on his way.

However, although the offer of agistment had been a ploy to enable the Joneses to get a week away, it was a godsend to us. Cyril watched him turn out of the gate, and amble from view.

"Yes, Mr. Jones," he thought to himself. "Good it is! I should have 'MUG' stamped across my forehead. You took me in, good and proper."

He reflected a moment.

"I think it was worth it," he grinned to himself. Although he'd laboured to bring thousands of gallons of water up from the beck, in exchange our little flock would get free grazing for several weeks.

CHAPTER THIRTEEN

As hay time approached, Cyril not only measured up the ings grass with an admiring eye, he also began to look covetously at the growth on the verge of Hagg Lane, which led to the main road. This verge was equally the width of the roadway and bore a rich crop of grass and clover.

While, on the farms which surrounded us, our neighbours began to overhaul their balers and the local agricultural engineer's van sped up and down the lanes from one to another, Cyril prepared for haymaking in a rather different fashion. Now that there was more grass to cut, he had progressed from the scythe he'd used to cut the orchard at 'Rose Dene.' Not far, however.

His latest farming 'mod con.' certainly wasn't modern, but would, we hoped, prove to be convenient. Far from being newfangled, our grass-reaper dated from pre-war days. It had been made originally for use behind horses. Sometime in its life, somebody had shortened the pole and put on an attachment to connect it to a tractor.

It had cost only a few pounds at a farm auction but, old as it was, Cyril had high hopes that it would make his work easier and quicker. Was it because of this labour-saving device that he now looked on the roadside grass with eyes of desire, or was it the old land-hunger once more coming to the surface?

Whatever it was, Cyril was determined that the roadside grass would form part of his stock of winter hay. There was, in Cottingwith itself, an ancient custom known as the 'Letting of the Lanes.' Each spring, the Parish Council auctioned off the grazing rights of certain lanes on the outskirts of the village. However, the lanes of Storwood didn't come under the jurisdiction of this body, so Cyril had no chance of bidding for them.

The taller the grass grew, the more eager he became to turn it into hay. At last, he strolled next door, to seek the brothers' advice.

"Oh, get it cut when the time comes," urged one.

"It'll only go to waste if you don't," added his brother.

"Do you think it's legal?" Cyril asked.

"Of course," they assured him. "The Council only cuts the main road and this in Hagg Lane grows so high that it's a nuisance to motorists."

135

With this salve to his doubts, he came back, full of excitement. Nothing would suffice but that we should take a walk along the lane to contemplate the amount of grass available, and to assess its "cuttability," so to speak. The land was by no means level, and would need care, but there was far more than we'd envisaged, never having examined it closely.

"If we can get this, as well as our own, we shall be all right for hay all winter," gloated Cyril, as we walked back home.

A few days later, he had a 'phone call from the owner of the Grange, a large farmhouse which stood in a lane which went off at right angles from Hagg Lane.

"The lads tell me you're going to cut the verge in Hagg Lane," he said. "I wonder if you'd cut ours?"

Cyril was over the moon. There were wide verges at each side of the little lane, and this would about double his hay crop.

Eventually, he decided to make a start. Not wanting to look too much of a fool, he began by cutting our own ings land, where he was safely out of sight of any passers-by. Coupling up the grass-reaper behind his trusty old Ferguson tractor, he went round and round the ings. The blades of the reaper chattered in their scissor-like action, and the grass fell in neat rows behind as he moved over the meadow.

"Come and look at this," he said, proudly, when I arrived home. "It's a good crop."

"All we need now is a fine, dry spell, and it should soon be safely led," I remarked.

The following day, he started to cut the roadside grass, much to the amusement of all who passed down the lane. While the fields were full of gleaming monsters, hurrying about their business and leaving the bales of hay strewn about the ground like dark green paper parcels, Cyril trundled slowly and carefully along the roadside with his antiquated machine. Of necessity, he went up the lane cutting the grass and then, lifting the blade, came back to his starting point and set off again.

"They can laugh," he told me, "but given dry weather, my hay will be just as good as theirs, if not better."

By the time he'd finished cutting, the hay on the ings was ready for turning and raking into windrows. I remembered hay-making as one of the pleasures of our early married life. The rhythm of the work and the scent of the hay brought a satisfaction which, to me, epitomised life on a farm.

We worked together, raking four rows of grass into one, to make a long, soft fluffy row, through which the wind could pass, to help the drying of the hay. We were mainly silent, enjoying the companionship and the closeness to nature.

"If it stays as warm as this, it'll be ready for putting into cocks by tomorrow," remarked Cyril with satisfaction as we packed up at dusk.

The new methods of farming may be quick but, to our way of thinking, you can't beat the old ways. It's quick and tidy to bale hay but, in Cyril's opinion, it hasn't the scent and flavour of hay made by the old-fashioned methods. The weather remained fine and sunny so that, after a couple of days in windrows, he was able to go along and gather up his hay into haycocks. Despite the banter of some local farmers, he was exceedingly proud of his hay-making.

"How long does it stay in those?" asked one young farmer, who had stopped his car to have a word and watch Cyril raking up the hay into cocks.

"It's led as soon as possible, as long as it's dry. You wasted three years at that Agricultural College!"

"They didn't teach us a lot about haycocks," he grinned.

"No! You'd be lost if oil disappeared overnight," retorted Cyril. "Your machines would be useless, but I could farm this way with a good horse."

With a cheery wave, the young man drove off — another acquaintance who'd labelled us as 'crackers.' Cyril was now impatient for us to begin leading. We'd been blessed with good weather, but it couldn't last for ever, and yet it would take both of us to do the work. When I arrived home on the Friday, he had the trailer connected up to the tractor and a couple of hay forks laid across it. Everything was ready for a quick start.

We more or less bolted our tea, and then I changed into trousers and off we went. We'd already decided to start leading from the furthest point. This was not only in case the weather broke before we finished leading the hay, in which case that which needed to be re-spread and dried out would be easier to reach. It was also because we'd no idea how our stamina would stand up and so, if we were tired, the remaining hay would be nearer the buildings.

Not possessing a Dutch barn and, let's face it, not really having enough hay to put in it if we had one, Cyril had cleared an open-fronted implement shed to hold the crop. This was situated in the stackyard field and had held the usual impedimenta of years of farming — bits of machinery, pieces of wood, oil drums and various other miscellaneous items. As we'd never needed the building, it had never been cleared, but Cyril had now got rid of the lot. The barn now stood ready and waiting — even the earth floor had been swept. Off we went!

I sat on the trailer, clutching a hay fork in each hand, as we bumped up the lane. When we pulled up at the farthest haycock, I jumped off and waited for Cyril to turn the tractor round. When he returned, I stood at the ready, grasping my fork in what I hoped was a businesslike way.

"We could really do with another pair of hands," Cyril remarked, "I shall spend half my time climbing on and off the tractor." I climbed back on the trailer and stood waiting.

"Keep it well out to the sides," instructed Cyril, as he passed up a forkful of hay. I felt quite expert as I gathered it from his fork to mine, and placed it in position on the trailer. I turned with a self-satisfied smirk, only to see him waiting with another forkful.

"I must be a bit quicker and get a rhythm going," I thought. Alas for my good intentions. As I tried to speed up the action, my forkful shot off the tines and down into the road at the other side of the trailer.

"I'm sorry, love. I've dropped it," I apologised.

"Putting it up once is enough, without having to do it twice!" admonished Cyril. "If you do it again, you'll have to get down and get it yourself."

Although I knew he was teasing, I could see that my carelessness would slow down the work.

Before long, of course, we established a rhythm, and I found it easier to position the hay where I wanted it. As each haycock was loaded, Cyril moved the tractor forward to the next, and we continued as before. I now began to feel a distinct unease, as the load grew higher. I've normally a good head for heights, but the trailer of hay wasn't expertly loaded, I must admit, and shifted slightly beneath my feet as I moved round it.

"Have we enough for this load?" I asked, trying to sound nonchalant.

Cyril studied it.

"No, we can get another couple of haycocks on."

To me, standing on top, it seemed quite high enough, but he was the boss. By the time we'd a full load it was beginning to grow dusk, a fact for which I was to be thankful. I wouldn't really have liked our progress along the lane to be exposed to public gaze.

To begin with, all went well. Cyril drove the tractor, singing at the top of his voice, while I sat atop the load, joining in. As we swung round into Hagg Lane, however, I felt the load shift beneath me.

Filled with consternation, I spread-eagled myself across it, trying to hold it together with my fingers and toes. Cyril sang away lustily, completely oblivious to the precarious position of his load — and his wife too, for that matter. Suddenly I felt the hay in the region of my feet falling away. I slid backwards to try to hold it, but suddenly found myself slithering down into the road, where I landed unceremoniously on a pile of hay.

It was lucky for me that enough had come off to soften my fall. Picking myself up quickly, I ran after the trailer, passed it, and came alongside the tractor, waving madly and shouting.

"Where have you come from?" he demanded.

"I fell off!"

"Fell off? How? Are you O.K.?"

"Yes, but there's a pile of hay in the road, I'm afraid."

As we walked back, I explained what had taken place.

"Don't worry, lass. We all have to learn," consoled my husband, as he gathered it up with his fork and threw it up on to the load. "Come and stand on the tow-bar, with your hands on my shoulders. We haven't far to go now."

We left the trailer backed into the barn, ready to be unloaded next day. This was a job that could be left, to fill in the time in the morning until the dew dried and we could lead more hay.

Saturday's leading went more smoothly, as I became quicker and more deft in my handling of the loose hay. I became quite expert in the way I took it form Cyril's fork on to mine, and placed it correctly on the trailer. As we unloaded more into the barn, this became the more tiring job.

The day was a scorcher and in the barn it was dark and hot, with the trailer pulled up in front blocking light and air. We were determined to finish if at all possible, believing that the weather was about to break. The air had become still and the atmosphere was almost thundery in its heaviness. During the afternoon, we were thankful to see Martin's van coming down the lane.

"We thought we'd come and give you a hand," he called, as he passed the tractor and trailer, and then drove into the fold-yard.

"Good," grunted Cyril, pausing to mop his brow with his forearm. "We should get finished now."

What a difference two extra pairs of hands made! The baby, Poppy, was put in her carrycot in the shade of a tree, with little Tammy picking flowers nearby, to keep an eye on her. We were now well down the lane and whoever was on top of the load could easily see in the stackyard field, to see that all was well. With Martin driving the tractor, Cyril loading, and Lesley and I forking up to him, things went well. By tea-time, we'd finished in the lane and only the ings remained. While I prepared tea, they stored the rest of the hay from the lane, and when he came in Cyril was delighted.

"There's about twice as much from the roadsides as I ever expected," he announced. "A grand crop it is, as well."

While Cyril brought in the goats, milked and fed the rest of the stock, we made a start on the ings. At least here we were free of the comments of passers-by, who seemed to regard us as some kind of hill-billies, with our old-fashioned methods.

"They can think what they like," I thought, "We've enough good hay to last over the winter."

Later in the evening, when we were alone, Cyril and I went up to the barn and surveyed the hay-crop. The barn was full, and the scent of the hay came to us on the night air. Cyril heaved a sigh of satisfaction.

"I'm really proud of this lot," he remarked, "We shall have no hay to buy in this winter, and it's all by our own efforts."

As I made to go back to the house, he put an arm round my shoulders. "Come on, lass. It's a lovely evening. Let's have a walk down on the bank."

As we strolled down the lane, I smiled.

"They all think we're crackers," I said, not for the first time.

"They can think what they like," said Cyril.

"I think we enjoy our farming more than they do theirs."

"There's one thing, love," he commented, "We can relax now. The moon's coming up and it's lovely and peaceful here."

It was indeed. The ducks and water-hens were quiet. The water moved smoothly in the half-light and only the occasional croak of a frog disturbed the silence.

"All the stock's fed, the hay's safely gathered in. If this moment

140

was in a game of 'Pontoon,' I'd stick," he murmured. He gave a grin, "Until the next crisis," he added.

At that moment, we heard the rumble of thunder in the distance. "Come on, love, or the next crisis will be upon us!"

With that, we turned and headed contentedly for home.